Lost in the Hive

Confessions of a Reluctant Drone

Brian O'Mara-Croft

Thanks for getting "lost"

PW

PublishingWorks, Inc.
2010

PublishingWorks, Inc.,
151 Epping Road
Exeter, NH 03833
603-778-9883
603-772-7200
www.publishingworks.com

Distributed to the trade by Publishers Group West

Designed by Anna Pearlman

LCCN: 2009907342
ISBN: 1-935557-08-4
ISBN-13: 978-1-935557-08-1

Printed on recycled paper.

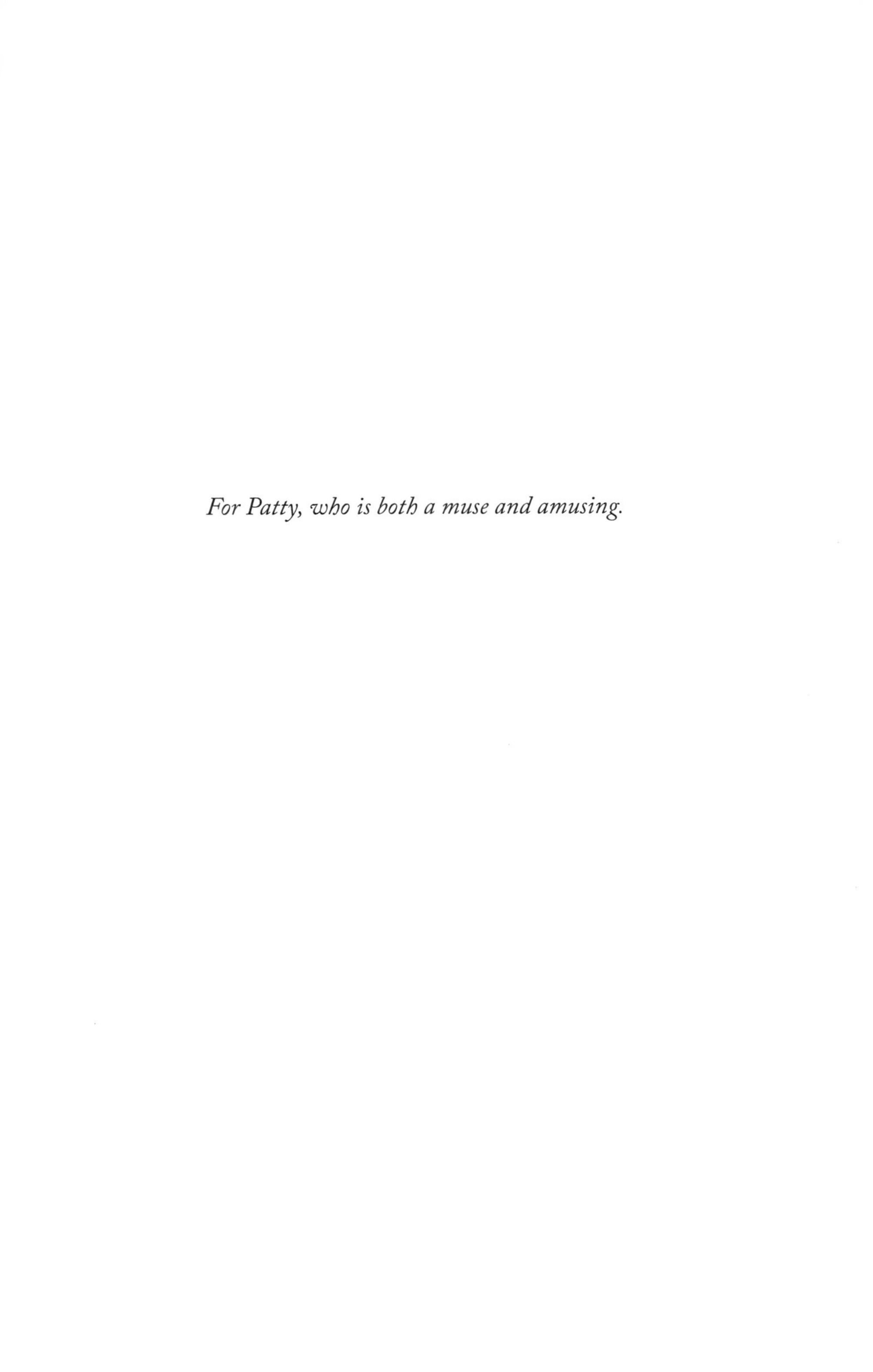

For Patty, who is both a muse and amusing.

Acknowledgments

I am grateful to a great many people who inspired the stories in this book, and who have shown boundless support for my desire to make others laugh, even if at times it was at their expense. First I must thank my wonderful wife Patty and my five children—Devin, Patrick, Colin, Kelly and Connor—whose love, devotion and good humor pervade both my life and the stories from it.

Thank you also to Neil, Kiddo, Weenie, Kevin, Dave, Mom, Dad, Paul, Der, Eemoolee, Count Varga, and the rest of my friends and family, who kept me believing a dream could come true.

Thank you to Carol, Abby, Anna, Kieran and the rest of the crew of PublishingWorks, with a special thanks to Jeremy for laughing in bed at early drafts of these stories.

And a from-the-bottom-of-my-heart thank you to my agent, Claire, for tolerating my rants and whines, and for keeping me focused, optimistic and real.

Thanks too to anyone I may have forgotten—I blame progressing age and substance abuse. I love you all.

Author's Note

The stories in this book are based on actual events as I recall them. I have changed the names of certain individuals so they don't track me down and beat me senseless. In some instances, I have compressed timeframes, or combined situations where telling all the details would turn this book into a 800-page behemoth.

The Stories

A Drone Before the Queen

Like many not-so-dangerously-handsome men whose hopes of gracing the cover of *People's* Sexiest Man Alive issue long ago fell into the giant compost heap of what-could-never-have-been-and-sure-as-hell-won't-happen-now, I often drift into whimsical daydreams. I can't help it. With two marriages spanning what now seems an astonishingly long adult life, and five precocious spawn either sired or acquired along the way, I relish these zesty fantasies. Hell, I live for them.

Lo and behold my brave and banal new dream world. Please don this complimentary raincoat; we keep it wet in here. In this realm, every remote control button launches a buffet of hardcore smut, year-round baseball, or novelty hybrids like porn baseball (where the seventh inning stretch is can't-miss entertainment). I try to watch, but miss a lot; my wife insists upon sexual excesses that would send the Marquis de Sade shrieking away. ("You want me to put what where? And how does this six pack of ginger ale figure into things? And why does that ferret look so angry?")

In my personal nirvana, I think nothing of indulging my twenty-seventh beer of the afternoon; I'll never suffer for it, and everyone will rejoice at my witty, drunken banter.

"It's just so adorable the way you call me a 'pudding pig,'" they'll say, and I'll wink as I tuck into my eighth Double Whopper. I'll then revel in the adulation of thousands who regard my ballooning beer paunch as a symbol not of excess but of gutsy stick-to-itiveness.

One recurring dream figment sees our chaotic home functioning less like an open bar at an Anarchists' League mixer and more like a serene, orderly, and industrious beehive. No, not dripping from wall to wall and across the ceiling in wax and honey—imagine trying to draw *that* out of lace curtains with an all-seeing queen buzzing about—but instead a cohesive colony in which each knows his place and stays there at all times.

What would that even be like? Was there really ever a time when children spoke only when spoken to, and were "seen but not heard?" I picture a giant army of diminutive mutes, eyes void of life, communicating through a primitive series of gestures, nods, and gesticulations—like interpretive dance, or awkward, uninspired foreplay. In my head, this is Heaven.

Parents of previous generations were brilliant—heartless, to be sure, but brilliant. Somehow, they cooked up a rule that allowed them to say whatever they wanted—and much was top-notch, my-Mommy-never-loved-me, thousands-in-future-therapy material—and the hapless victim could do nothing but stand there and take it, over and over, like a Weeble with a quivering lip. Pure magic.

Today, children are both seen (too often) *and* heard (*far* too often). Some prattle on even amid subtle cues not to, like, "By all that is holy, for just one millisecond, would you please, please, *please* shut the hell up?" I'm clearly of the wrong generation; was it that long ago we parents lost our right to smite? Isn't there a freaking commandment to fall back on?

In my dream hive, we'd depart from convention and allow not only for a dominant queen—some things are a given, even in dreams—but also an omnipotent, greatly feared, yet much-adored, King Bee. That's where I come in.

My worker bees—all of whom would bear quirky names like Buzz and Pollen—would without question do the bidding that befits one of such royal lineage. They'd be happy to shut the hell up, out of an instinctive need to coddle and placate. Besides, with no vocal chords, how much real complaining could they do? Let them buzz all they want; I've mastered the art of ignoring repetitive background sounds, like the ominous hums and cries of anguish from our washing machine. These are now a mechanical lullaby, as unobtrusive as the gentle whirr of a ceiling fan. I now live by a simple formula:

explosion or fire (or chance for sex) = now
anything else = later

"Buzz, fetch me a ridiculous amount of Honeycomb." In my dream world, there are no luxuries like question marks or the word *please.* As if by magic, a colossal bone china mixing bowl would appear, cereal heaped over the top, the surface tension of the milk defying gravity across the rim. This bounty would arrive on a gold platter with fine linens, a beeswax candle, and a chilled chalice (also gold) of Honey Wheat Ale to wash the works down. I realize the combination sounds vile; when you're King Bee, indulge your own whimsies. Wear a Speedo to the office, if you're convinced you look hot in it (you don't). Go to your local drive-thru and repeatedly order the wrong things, since you know you'll never receive what you ask for anyway. When someone in front of you ambles along too slowly, follow your heart and sucker-punch that person in the back of the head—hard, like there's a prize to be won if the skull comes off. If you're going to dream, dream big.

In a real hive, the male bees, or drones, pretty much do nothing. About this I need not daydream—we've achieved this in real life.

Our four drones (five, if you include me, and the Queen certainly would) are masters of sloth, content to bask through days and nights in their own squalor.

The basement of our present hive, in which two of our adult sons have crafted a makeshift bedroom/landfill, should have a bare floor. Instead, it bears a crude carpet of HoHo wrappers scattered inexplicably around the near-empty garbage pail, back issues of *Maxim* with the pages sealed together (I suspect from a dark variety of teenage multitasking), filthy socks (see multitasking above), and stains that might once have been food and then again might not. Chocolate it may well be, but *I'm* not doing any sniff tests. The whole room exudes a heady aura of dirty feet, stale cigarettes, sour milk and teenage angst.

One morning, my wife found a Cool Whip container on our kitchen counter. Inside was a panicked frog. As you might expect, she asked, "Hey, what's this panicked frog doing on the kitchen counter?" And then, "When did we buy Cool Whip?" Strange she didn't react with more alarm, as though on any given day one might expect to find a jailed toad, newt, or salamander where we normally fix sandwiches.

With some sleuthing we discovered that, during the night, our son had heard the intruder rustling through the garbage he'd stuffed under his brother's bed during the last Mom-ordered room cleaning. His mother and I beamed with pride—how many kids can boast they've sired their own ecosystem? With said container was a note offering, simply, "I punched no holes. I hope it dies."

Drones One and Three reside in Canada with my first and former queen bee, and fly south a few times each year. Drone One, in typical twenty-year-old fashion, flits from place to place, not yet sure where or what he wants to be, nor what color, length, or style of hair he'll sport when he arrives. We've pictured him as actor, chef, game designer, world adventurer, pool-boy/gigolo, and comic book superhero. Will the world ever be the same once Fondue Boy soars with locks of aquamarine and an all-seeing eye above our streets, alleys, mountains, and plains?

Drone Three, eighteen, would answer "to bee or not to bee" with a resounding "not to," because if everyone else is a bee, he must be a wasp, yellow jacket, or hornet—anything but a plain ol' stinking bee. Fame, to him, is another word for "selling out." Air conditioning is a dangerous throwback to fascism. And watching us spray ants with Raid seems too close to ethnic cleansing. He'll introduce us to a new song and, if we like it, will then say, "You do? Yeah, well, it sucks." This streak of individuality both endears and (more often) aggravates.

Drones Two and Four share our daily hive. Drone Two, nineteen, is our most self-assured member, the "me" bee. There's little in the world he doesn't already claim to know, and few things he could improve upon by following others' advice. On his Facebook page he claims to have visited places he has only *flown over* en route to other, less-exotic destinations. He even lists Ireland among his travels. Unless he stole out of our home at night, stowed away on Aer Lingus, toured the Emerald Isle in seven minutes, and found his way back to his bed before daybreak, methinks he's spinning a bit of a tale. He's never been overseas, but some of his cousins have—that's close enough. He's worldly by association.

"Son, take cover, the sky is falling."

"I know." He *always* knows. "Except it's not really falling in the purest scientific sense. It's sagging, and may one day hemorrhage and, naturally, because of gravity, would fall toward Earth. That's simple physics; you didn't know that?" I rarely know, or care. We feel some anxiety a cruel world may one day fall upon our resident expert, but he'd come through it like Atlas, supporting the world upon his shoulders until, tired, he'd set the Earth down and forget where he left it.

Drone Four, fourteen, is the polar opposite of Two. He's cautious, reserved, sensitive, petrified of change, and madly curious about the inane details of everyday life. He's our busy bee. I adore him when he's asleep; when he starts asking questions, as he does through each waking moment, I understand why kidnapers duct tape hostages' mouths. He's relentless. Were there in fact a medical condition called verbal diarrhea, we'd be cleaning up giant, steaming piles of words everywhere.

"When the phone rings and it's an unknown caller, who's on the phone? Why are the curtains open today when they were closed yesterday? When people look smaller on the TV screen, are they really smaller? I see you're sitting there talking—so, what are you doing—just sitting there talking? Why did the birds eat all the food in the feeder? Will it be sunny or rainy twelve weeks from now?"

If I told this one the sky was falling, he'd dive for cover and ask, "After the sky falls, will there still be clouds?"

Female bees are the workers, whose primary focus in life is to serve and protect the queen, and to maintain a tidy hive. Alas, my sole daughter falls well short of this ideal. Even at seventeen she's convinced *she's* the heir apparent. Instead of the "royal jelly" bees bestow upon the future monarch of a hive, we've substituted four thousand dollars' worth of skin-care products, pure mineral makeup and jewelry, and dresses donned only once (twice if you count the requisite pre-event preening session) and then relegated to the deep recesses of the closet. When I dare challenge her request for new clothes with, "But you just got a new dress," her eyes snap back into her cranium, zombie-like, and through the back of her head I hear, "What-eh-ver. I'll just talk to Mom."

She says this last word in such a way its counterpart—Dad—is synonymous with "shithead loser."

And watch out for the stinger on this one—cloaked during her softer moments, it can appear with lightning speed the second anyone invades her kingdom. This includes her bedroom (from the doorknob of which dangles a sign with hearts and stars and fuzzy bunnies and a friendly warning: "Stay Out!"), and what we've tried and failed to assert is the kids' (plural) bathroom. Of course, she feels no qualms about helping herself to anything and everything in Mom and Dad's bathroom, because our shouted order, "Kelly, listen carefully—you must not *ever* go into our bathroom again," was too ambiguous.

Just the other day, our daughter's room was a scaled-down replica of a CNN feature on the latest heartrending act of God—missing only a few bloated corpses floating past on driftwood—yet she complained with great shrieks and machinations about the cleaning ladies messing her space up when they removed a full metric ton of clothing from her floor.

"Mom, hurry! You just *have* to see this. Oh no, oh my God, they've *moved* stuff around. They moved *everything!* Can't you please just fire them? Are they even allowed to be in this country? I mean, they've changed it *all*." And the Emmy for best actress in a dramatic role goes to . . .

Given my choice, our hive would not look too, well, hive-like. That might attract unwanted critical attention. Like the garage door I once saw where the owners had reproduced, in painstaking detail, da Vinci's "The Last Supper." I imagine the rapturous smile on the husband's face as a religious icon gradually unfolds before him—first the sandaled feet, then the white tablecloth, the dinner rolls, and plates, and at last the king of kings himself. Then I relish his look of sheer horror when an errant Tickle Me

Elmo in the line of the sensor unceremoniously rolls the Son of God and his devoted crew back up into the heavens. He is arisen, pal; he is not here.

Aside from the distinctive shape of a hive, which might seem a tad garish in an otherwise boxy and characterless suburban landscape, the color could pose a problem. Brilliant gold brick, siding, and shutters, along with the perching of our home high up a mature tree, would be sure to lead our more particular neighbors to bitch and moan.

"Hey, Earl, come look at this. Earl!" If you've ever watched *Bewitched*, or ever had a mother-in-law, you know this voice, which sounds like the screech of a burning cat clipped to a barbed-wire clothesline. "That's not a house! *That*, Earl . . . " And she'd pause, just like that, to make sure Earl was suitably appalled, "That is a seventeen-hundred-square-foot gob of bling." Earl, for his part, would just nod and agree in silence, all the while planning to chop the harpy's nattering body into thousands of steak-sized chunks.

So if we're to have a hive, we'll need to settle on a more-subtle, restrained approximation of one. But there's little room for subtleties in our hive, I'm afraid. Oh, if only we didn't have so many rogue bees. And such an authoritative queen.

In our hive, my wife Patty is a split-personality sort of bee. First and foremost, she *is* the queen. Few dare to dispute this, except perhaps our aforementioned queen-in-waiting. Whenever I've deigned to claim I wear the pants, my friends first snicker and then remark between guffaws, "She lets you wear pants?" What Patty doesn't achieve through royal pronouncements she gains by wearing us lesser bees down.

"Just how much more stuff do you think you could store on top of the TV armoire, honey? Would you like me to move the votive holders to make room for more books and magazines? Here, let me stack your wallet and cell phone up there, too. Aw, that looks just darling." When she then adds, "Don't you think?" I'm pretty sure she's being insincere. And when she says, "Now get rid of it," I'm certain. Wow, who knew queen bees were such masters of biting sarcasm? Of course, King Bee or not, I now have an unwanted errand to accomplish, with nary a worker bee in sight. I remain a mere drone, and need only ask the queen to affirm this.

And yet our queen is also our most dedicated worker bee, buzzing here and there to re-accomplish things already addressed—except they'll be done right this time, a concept it seems only the queen can grasp. You can scour our kitchen until it shines so profoundly the crew of the shuttle Endeavour would need sunglasses to regard it from space, and still Patty will discover (and rail against) the lone miniscule spatter of oil under the bottom lip of the countertop. And if anyone eases a dish into the left side of the sink (the "reserved" side, for some reason), she can hear the clink from the Target store two miles away. The phone will blare, and then she'll blare, "Who just put something into the left sink?" She must have some form of hyper-attuned sensor for these things—perhaps her furry antennae?

As much as my daydream of beedom appeals, some qualities of this culture I would find hard to bear. For one—honeybees communicate through a series of movements called the waggle dance. I'm a white, middle-aged male, more WASP than bee in my coordination. Everyone knows white men can't jump, and even fewer, I believe, can waggle. I'm among this group. Try as I might, I can't get my feeble brain and even-more-feeble limbs to move in sync with music. I look like I've had a sudden, shuddering four-minute-long chill, or like I'm miming a stroke in progress.

What's more, I'm forever catching myself falling into the

cliched but entirely instinctive habit of extending my top teeth over my bottom lip—the dreaded white man's overbite. I make this same face during sex, although few similarities exist between dancing and lovemaking, other than that I'm winded after doing either for a short period of time . . . that, and I don't do either very well.

So if I'm ever forced to communicate through a series of flailings and quasi-obscene gyrations, I'll forever be fostering confusion.

"Just what are you trying to say, Brian? You're suffering from walnut-sized hemorrhoids? You think you're spontaneously combusting? You'd like me to suffocate you in your sleep?" I don't have the faintest idea where she came up with the last one, but it's offered often.

Another challenge: every honeybee colony bears a unique odor, so that the more dim-witted or nectar-drunk bees who forget their own address can still sniff their way home. (This must work, because when drink makes me forget how to walk I still stagger in the proper direction before collapsing on the front lawn.)

Our queen, unfortunately, isn't a big fan of most odors, except on those rare occasions when I pick up an impromptu bunch of roses or a rotisserie chicken. She hates when I don't flush the toilet after peeing, regardless of how many times I've dragged out tired sayings like, "If it's yellow, let it mellow." Her response is fresh and lively: "Your piss I smell, so go to hell."

I seldom pan-fry seafood anymore. Being told my food makes the whole house smell like shit somehow tempers both my appetite and my enthusiasm. And my queen gets downright testy when I offer up a personal scent in bed, particularly if I quickly snap the covers up and over her head to concentrate its hearty nuances (the much-ballyhooed Dutch Oven, perfectly executed). Some queens just can't take a joke.

The final deviation I'd make from bee society—and this is a big one—relates to mating. Queen bees are shameless sluts. They'll happily hook up with a dozen or more partners in a short-lived orgiastic free-for-all. Call me old-fashioned, but I regard this as counterproductive to a happy marriage. I'd prefer we continue to buzz in our own backyard.

Were that not enough, the act itself is a trifle alarming. When each male bee finishes his happy task (*buzz . . . buzz . . . buzz . . . buzzzz . . .*), he can't instantly roll over and commence sawing logs (*zzzz . . .*). He doesn't have to cuddle the queen to convince her he's not selfish, but the fate awaiting him is far worse. In a strange twist that further makes me question the existence of a supreme being, his genitals *snap off* inside the female. Said genitals are called an endophallus, which, if pronounced phonetically, seems ironically and tragically appropriate. The rest of this poor sap's now-dead body (since he now has no good reason to live, as far as I'm concerned) plummets to the earth. I want no part of this. Not only do I not want to lose my treasured stinger, especially in a snapping fashion, I most certainly don't want my last deed to be to add it to a pile of others.

As I revel in these fancies, I wonder if I could ever truly be King Bee, lord and master of my humble domain. Would the queen and queen-in-waiting ever share the throne, or will I continue to provoke them into stinging rages? Will I ever waggle dance without looking like a drunken beaver in the throes of a *grand mal?* And why am I asking so many questions like Drone Four? I don't know the answers, so I dream and dream. It's the least I can do. As a reluctant drone before an all-powerful, all-seeing queen, it's really all I can do.

Shoo Fly Try

Whenever a fly visits our home, which is often, our entire life switches channels—from the saccharin serenity of *The Brady Bunch* to one of the more surreal episodes of *The Outer Limits*. On cue, Carol Brady sheds her calm, suburban veneer, and from the discarded husk bursts a raging, drooling she-creature. Mike Brady would be the first to tell you an enduring marriage is built on triumphs over adversity, but he'd never have found time to design buildings or shoot the shit with Don Drysdale if forced to spend his days tending to the insect-fueled furies of a Carol Beast. Such is my frequent plight.

"There's a fly in here," Patty/Carol Beast booms, with equal parts terror and disgust, as though she expects it to light on her body, sweep her off, and force her to serve as mother and queen to a sea of writhing, ravenous maggots. I try to ignore her. A Madagascar hissing cockroach or African giant millipede might capture my attention, but a lone fly isn't worth leaving my chair for. Besides, since the average fly seldom lives more than three weeks, I'm prepared to wait him out.

"Aren't you going to get it?" So now it's *my* fly.

"Quick, getit getit getit. It's on the chair. No, now it's flying again. It's on the curtain. Aren't you going to . . . Brian! Getit getit getit!" From two rooms away, I can hear her head flipping back and forth, up and down, tracking.

"Okay, honey, just give me a minute." I think if I employ a stall tactic, Patty may forget, and Carol Brady will ease back into her human skin. No. Patty never forgets about flies. Or mosquitoes. Or moths. Or dust bunnies . . . even cute ones, like the ones the cleaning ladies always miss under the TV cabinet. We may sit around all day waffling about things to do, but if one common housefly (*musca domestica*) drops in, we become singular of purpose.

"But, honey, there's a fly in here. I can feel it buzzing me." Not content to feast on the crumbs and endless sticky spots in the adjoining kitchen, these flies dine only on skin cells, moisturizer, and my wife's unbridled rage. I'm going to have to get up.

I sigh. "Okay, just a second."

"Where's the flyswatter? Get the flyswatter, will you?" I've taken too long. "Oh, never mind, I'll get it." She storms to the fridge and reaches up and back, beyond the cereal, where we keep a battery-powered electric device that can bring even the swiftest of flies right out of the air. The FlyFucker 2000, a weapon of mass destruction that hums and crackles as it comes to life. It doesn't just kill flies; it incinerates them. Patty likes this.

Except it isn't there. Nor is the second garden-variety backup swatter I had purchased to prevent scenes like this. Nor is the third. Now, I'm mobilized. We've reached DEF CON One.

"Where's the freaking flyswatter? Who took it? The flyswatter isn't where it's supposed to be!" I could add italics to every word, because each drips with fury and more than a hint of menace. She screams for each of the children and lays into them like the drill sergeant from *Full Metal Jacket*. Nobody has a clue, just as they never know what happened to the tab from the bread, why all the cookies mysteriously dropped into another dimension, or who tossed two AA batteries on the lawn to boil in the sun. At this point, even if they have the flyswatter, they dare not admit it; ignorance at such times is most certainly bliss. She sends them off with, "If you get sick because of the flies, don't blame me," and resumes the hunt.

Emboldened and unusually perceptive, the fly lands on Patty's arm, twitches its wing, and looks at her, unblinking. Do flies smile? Its flippant gesture, its mere existence is, to Patty, an all-out declaration of war.

"What the hell! Did you just see that? He just landed right on my arm!" I doubt I would respond this strongly if it landed right on my tongue, but Patty's distress is palpable.

"Get a magazine. Just get a magazine and kill that thing before it lands on me again." Flies carry close to two million different strains of bacteria. In their lifetime, they can give birth to three thousand fresh new flies, taking a break from eating and fornicating just long enough to take a dump every five minutes. Patty is utterly convinced all of these things have just happened on her arm. She shudders, and then runs to the bathroom to scour herself, à la Karen Silkwood. I pick up her new *People* magazine. If I actually kill the fly with the magazine, I'll be obliged to put a mist of Windex on a paper towel and wipe it off, but only if she sees me.

"It's in here! Oh my God, it's in the bathroom." She slams the door. "Don't come in. It's cornered." I can hear small, swift whiffs of wind and breathless expletives as she flails around the tiny room, another magazine in hand. She implores her foe to land, but it doesn't listen; from what I understand, flies seldom do.

A few seconds later, a sharp slapping sound, and an enormous cry of triumph.

"Yes! Take that, you stupid-ass fly!"

Toilet paper spins off the roll—a lot of it—and then the toilet flushes, a whirling celebration of death. The magazine, now worthless, falls into the garbage. Patty emerges, beaming, handing out high fives to all, as though she had just mounted the podium at Beijing, gold in Singles Extermination.

Patty has made it her mission in life to dispatch as many flying insects as humanly possible. Just the other day, I delivered a glancing blow to yet another aggressive fly. Instead of dying outright, it fell in the sink and spun in circles, like a break-dancer. On some occasions, Patty might pull up a chair and savor each of the many death throes. This time, though, she waved me off, like an outfielder calling for a pop-up, and shouted, "Stand back. I've got this one." Whereupon she grabbed the fifty-six-ounce bottle of Dawn detergent and power-squeezed at least one-eighth of the green goo directly onto the rapidly decelerating fly. She then washed the slippery but spotless fly corpse down the drain.

I once made the colossal mistake of play-swatting my wife on the behind with a flyswatter. I thought I was cute and flirtatious; I expected a wave of the hand and an equally cute, "Oh you." Maybe this hint at romance, followed by both cooking and cleaning up after dinner, would lead to some equally cute gestures on her part later in bed. No such luck. To Patty, I had inexplicably coated her jeans in fly feces.

"Why would you do that?" I recall this multi-purpose question; I've been asked it many times. "Ewww . . . you smeared fly guts all over me. Now I have to change. Oh my God. Please don't ever do that again." She walked gingerly upstairs, like a child with a full diaper, afraid to make contact with the clothes that were now so blatantly and brazenly soiled.

Patty bears no special prejudices against species of insects; they are all universally abhorrent. Every year, we experience a mini-infestation of ants, in part because of the constant opening and closing of doors, and in part because our garbage pail has a huge hole punched through at floor level—a veritable red carpet for ravenous critters. For all that our efforts at pest control have yielded, we might just as well go outside, grab great handfuls of ants, and throw them on the floor.

Now, Patty likes a clean floor. We don't even need to bother, most times, with five-second rules for dropped items; the floor is cleaner than the hand that dropped the food. If she steps on a crumb of stale oatmeal cookie, she recoils as if her toes had squished through a knee-deep, steaming pile of dog shit. These ants, to Patty, are moving crumbs, a disgusting obstacle course arranged, without permission, on oft-Swiffered linoleum. They're like neighbors that only show up when they're drunk. Only there because of what you're providing (booze or crumbs), they seem oblivious to your discomfort and stay so long you want to whack them with a shoe.

To be fair, Patty has some fair justification for her bias. Bar none, she is a favorite target of the insect world. It's not even subtle. In MosquitoLand (also known as our untended bird bath and the fifty-foot radius around it), Patty is a poster girl for fine dining. I can spend an entire evening by our backyard firepit and never see or hear a mosquito, and never worry about lightning bugs because, at night, they look like Christmas lights instead of the disgusting flies they are. Patty merely steps out the door and is beset by swarms, like John Coffey ("like the drink, but not spelled the same, ma'am") from *The Green Mile*. She could take a long soak in a tub of DEET, walk once around our yard, and by the next morning her face, her ears, her legs, her feet—even her fingers—look like oversized Braille. These aren't regular bumps, either; they're angry, oblong boils that itch without mercy.

It's not that we haven't taken up the fight. At any given time, we possess more than a half dozen different types of insect repellent, most designed for treks through the deep rainforest and certainly devastating to both skin and the respiratory tract. These have descriptors like extreme, ultra-hypertoxic, and genocidal on them. We have lanterns into which you insert a candle and a tab of insecticide-soaked fabric. Most people have one—we have many, a forest of torches surrounding our smallish patio.

Added to this arsenal is a handheld fogger that billows such great clouds of noxious smoke that after each use our backyard looks like a Van Halen concert. I make multiple passes across our property, making sure each bush, each blade of grass, and every breath of air is coated in death-administering richness. I'm temporarily blind, I smell like bad aftershave, and it's all for naught. By the time we go inside for the night, Patty is the before photo on one of those infomercials for industrial-strength acne medicine.

Discovery Channel airs a show called *Verminators*, in which a group of eccentric pest control technicians rid homes of rats, bats, roaches, black widow spiders, and countless other nasties that have taken over homes, attics, and gardens. This is a profession nobody could aspire to, but these lovable losers crack jokes and terrible puns while nature runs amok around them. I enjoy the show as a diversion; to Patty, it is evidence.

"Do you see? Do you see why I worry about the flies? If you let them in, they never, *ever* leave. It just gets worse and worse and worse, and next thing you know it's *The Amityville Horror*, with bloated stinking flies in your food, in your clothes, everywhere. Do you see?"

I don't see, really. Call me obtuse, but I see a vast difference between one fly and thirty rats, or even a single mouse—like the one that once took up residence in our glove compartment and made a nest of our owner's manual. (Of course, Patty made this discovery, with a rain of screams matched only in volume by the sudden squeal of brakes. Only when we more or less stripped the car of all of its contents, and I checked to make sure the mouse wasn't curled up, content, in her headrest, would she continue the ride.) To be fair, if a mouse runs into the room, I'm like the maid in the *Tom & Jerry* cartoons—a stereotype on tiptoes dancing on a kitchen chair. But a fly? A fly is an annoyance, an irritating drum riff as it bounces off the window, into the blinds, back against the window, around the window, off the blinds, and so on. But it's not a rat. When rats fly, I'll be an instant and total convert. I've tried this argument, but to no avail.

Patty watches, both thrilled and appalled, as the TV exterminators emerge with a glue trap bearing a rat the size of a puppy.

"I'd just leave. I wouldn't even take anything. I'd just be gone."

As she says this, a fly darts across the room and, like an Airbus, makes a broad sweeping turn before descending to a graceful landing on our coffee table. It looks right at Patty. I sigh, smile at her, and say, "Here, let me get that for you, dear," then reach for an imaginary zipper at the back of her head to again unleash the Carol Beast.

Hope Springs Eternal . . . and Early

"Brian? It's . . ."

I can't make it out; I was in a dead sleep, a slobbering coma. I think I heard "God," but He never calls anymore, because I'm far too liberal in using His name in vain. His kid Jesus doesn't fare much better; when I run into him next, I expect to hear, "Brian, do I call you Brian Fucking O'Mara-Croft? No? Well it's not my middle name either!"

I'm tentative, and cross myself for good measure. Into the phone I whisper, "God?"

"No, Brian, not God. Dad. Breakfast ready?"

My father *always* says this. He says this even though he knows that I'm such a dreadful host I wouldn't remember to offer coffee, towels, prostitutes, toilet paper, or fresh linens to sleepover guests, let alone bacon and eggs. Maybe that's why he says it.

I employ the back of my free hand to chip enough brittle crust from my eyes to decipher the digital clock. What is that first digit? An eight? No, a nine? Oh shit, it's a six! Someone must be horribly maimed, or even more horribly dead. I've been plucked from a dream in which I'm hand-tanning the buttocks of a very happy wife while she shrieks, "Captain, My Captain!" and begs to watch another football game with me. Oh, I guess we can; anything for you. Multiple football games, like strings of orgasms, almost never happen in real life—at least in my life. I'm now half-conscious, trying to make sense of the telephone in my hand. Did I even answer it?

"Dad . . . yeah . . . hey, what's wrong?"

Patty rolls over and flop-drapes an arm across my chest. This is her way of saying she's there for me if I receive irrefutable evidence hell is freezing over, but she'd prefer to be well rested for any imminent apocalypse. She's no doubt dreaming about a vacuum that not only picks up all the dust in the world, but locks it away forever in some other dimension—like those baddies in the Superman movies. I'm guessing rough sex has nothing to do with her dream, although I indulge an alpha sleep moment about using the Dyson's sofa attachment as a paddle. *You . . . will . . . not . . . clean. You . . . will . . . not . . . clean. Say it!*

My Dad's voice breaks my reverie.

"Oh, nothing. Your mother and I were just sitting here having our coffee and working out a few things."

"Oh, okay, cool. Talk to you later."

"No, wait. We may have some good news for you."

I perk up, just a touch. One eye is half-open, the other is trying to skulk back to the kink. What would qualify as good news? Creationists don T-shirts with a smiling T-Rex on the front and announce they were just kidding, that of course the fifty fucking million fossils we've found just might mean something? *There I go, angering God again.* What else? People the world over swear, upon penalty of death, never to again say "nucular"? That *would* be good news. My Dad tells me he's paying off my mortgage?

"Your mother and I were talking, and if—and we know this is a big if—we win the lottery this weekend, we think we could probably pay off your house."

Bing! . . . Oh.

Now I'm more awake. My parents are very generous people. My brothers and I would be sporting fancy new concrete high-tops at the bottom of Lake Ontario had they not bailed our sorry asses out of countless financial quagmires; these are kindnesses we'll never be able to pay back or forward. In a squeeze, my mom would give me the shirt off her back—but as her kid I'd prefer she kept it on. It hurts more than you'd think to poke out your mind's eye. But did I really hear what my father said?

"I'm sorry, Dad. Did you just say you're going to pay off our mortgage?"

"Well, no, not exactly. But Mom and I took out our budget book and . . ."

I don't even know what a budget book is. Bills come in, often. If there's money there, you pay a select few the last instant before your house plunges into darkness. If not, you toss them on the stack, the *big* stack, the most ignored item in our home (next to my requests for sex during non-bed hours). Sure, I want to get on the right track, but I'm forever forced to weigh the relative importance of say, water, against the seeming imperative of prime rib as the ground meat in my shepherd's pie.

"We looked at our numbers. If we win the twenty million, we can pay off our debts, replace our car, and come up with a few dollars to help you guys out."

If hope springs eternal for most of us, for my father it's a rabid, drooling jackrabbit on crystal meth. Don't get me wrong; optimism, in moderation, is a good thing. I too have fantasized about walking into a luxury car dealership and plunking down 265 large, cash, for a brand new Aston Martin DBS. Too few cars (and too many porn films) list "hand-finished" as one of their qualities.

But I know it will never, ever, ever, ever happen for me.

"Yeah, Dad. That's great. I have to go water my horse." Dads of his generation adore cute clichés like this; they sound so much more charming, I guess, than "gotta squirt." "Can I call you back later to talk about this?" I won't be calling back.

"Want to say hello to your mother?" Touché. The classic move, mastered by fathers the world over. Say what you have to say, then pass the baton before the conversation drifts into awkward personal stuff like, "Papa, why don't you ever give me whisker rubs anymore?"

"Well, son, it's because you're forty-two." I silently applaud his savvy. The student has not yet surpassed the master.

"Hello, dear. Did we wake you?" She knows she did.

"No. I was just reading a book." She knows I'm lying. This is their small measure of retribution for all the times when, as children, we would pound on their bedroom door during their Saturday afternoon "nap" and whine, "I'm hungry. What are you *doing* in there?"

I almost called them the night prior, after several cocktails, just to slur through the inane details of my day and to lay undeserved guilt for my childhood at their feet. It's called "drink and dial," and I'm the reigning champ. Put me on the phone sober and I'm as chatty as Helen Keller in handcuffs, but throw a few wobblies in me and I become the unwelcome life of even the worst parties. It's one of life's paradoxes: the more people struggle with their tongue and teeth, the more they're inclined to talk at length.

"Mom, do you remember that time I bought you the Zippo with the giraffe on it? Don't think I didn't see it, over and over, in the junk drawer. You never loved me!"

Still, a little voice told me that waking my parents when I was stinking drunk would only frustrate them enough to call me at 6:30 in the morning. *Good thing I didn't, huh?* Besides, a vague memory reminded me nothing positive ever comes from drinking and talking to your parents. Once, my brother had consumed one too many and "complimented" my Mom by offering, "Holy shit, Mom, even *you* have good legs when I'm drunk." I must have been a bit tipsy myself because I too checked them out and agreed with my brother's assessment. So I didn't call my parents.

I phoned my friend Chris instead; he drinks on much the same schedule, and at roughly the same pace, and is hopelessly bitter about many of the same things, so the three hours of love, repressed anger, and bitter tears went down with as little effort as my eighth whisky and Diet Coke.

"So, what do you think about your Dad's idea?" Mom asks.

Now I'm stuck. Call me a doubting Thomas, but I'm not yet convinced I'll be a Rockefeller heir before the weekend's out. I've read the statistics. The odds of winning the Mega Millions jackpot are about one in 175 million. Think about this: just over 300 million people live in this country. If my math is correct, and it probably isn't, I have about half as good a chance of walking into a bar in Waco, Texas, and running into the one person from Minneapolis who just happened to be on my mind as I walked through the door. A wise person doesn't plan a future around these odds.

According to some research I Googled, one of the only things less likely to happen is for an errant meteor to score a direct hit on your living room; *that* I'd gladly offer up my house for just to see. In the meantime, you could repel multiple attacks by ravenous mountain lions and have your nightwear burst spontaneously into flames many times over and still not have a penny to show for it. You could even become a saint. Well, I couldn't, but perhaps *you* could.

What's more, those who do hit the jackpot—usually toothless, bible-thumping hillbillies with names like Jed or Bud—don't always become *Beverly Hillbillies.* William "Bud" Post, who in 1988 won $16.2 million in the Pennsylvania lottery, lost a significant share of his winnings to an ex-girlfriend. Were it me, I would prefer to give an ex something non-monetary—say, syphilis—than to fork over millions to the person most likely to have me whacked. For Bud Post, his ex-girlfriend wasn't as much of a threat as his brother. Thinking he might be in the will, Bud's brother allegedly hired a hit man to take poor Bud out. And then things really went south. Bud invested in two failed businesses, spent time in jail for firing a gun over the head of a bill collector, racked up huge debt and ultimately declared bankruptcy. Given my track record with money, I'd fare little better than Bud. I'd sure like to try for a while, but I'm not hopeful about the outcome.

"Dad's idea's great, Mom. Uh . . ."

Do I say thank you? Isn't that a lot like seeing something your wife would like at the fine jewelry counter in Macy's and coming home to say, "You know what I *almost* bought you?"

"Well, I'll tell you one thing." She pauses to make sure I'm listening.

"Mmm?" I was drifting off. *Take that, sugar, and that! Who's your Captain?*

"We won't be *giving* you the money. We'll pay off your house, and we might help with your bills. But we're not just *giving* you a bunch of money. You'll just waste it."

It's true. If you gave me $200,000 today, I would waste some. Okay, I'd waste a lot. I've never had anything even approaching that much at my disposal, so I really would do something stupid, like travel to the Galapagos and smuggle a giant tortoise in my luggage. Or I might transform my backyard into a miniature replica of U.S. Cellular Field complete with sand infield, bleachers, hot dog stands, topless cheerleaders, and my new tortoise mascot, or buy five thousand lottery tickets just to see if lightning might strike twice (odds: one in nine million). But I'm in hot water with my mom for *not* spending the money she *didn't* give me? How fair is that? I try to plot an escape, but I'm not awake enough yet.

"Mom, I gotta run. The baby's crying."

"Nice try. You don't have a baby."

"The dog needs to go out." I'm reaching.

"You have a dog? You're lying—never in a million years would Patty go for that."

I feel cornered. Cold sweat beads my brow. Come on, man, come up with something!

"Um . . . um, oh my God! Oh my God! An engine from a plane just crashed into our front lawn!"

"Don't be silly. Do you know the odds of that happening?"

Exactly.

A Clean and Present Danger

This morning, I read with a curious mix of amusement and terror a police report about a twenty-year-old Texan woman who faces criminal charges for allegedly biting a chunk out of her boyfriend, smashing his face with a picture frame and attempting to lop his head off with a two-foot sword—all because he'd broken his promise to wash the dishes. Am I alone in thinking she may be overwrought? And would anyone fault the boyfriend if he emerged from this just a little more commitment-phobic?

Still, as I digested the details, I did a quick inventory—Patty most certainly has teeth; a substantial arsenal of picture frames of various sizes and materials graces our home; and, ironically, there's even an antique sword stashed in the back corner of our bedroom closet (I didn't put it there, so my anxiety was only heightened). Mere moments later, after securing all our family photos under lock and key, and putting a sign on the sword that read, "This is not a sword," I was elbows-deep in suds, scrubbing like Lady Macbeth and watching the clock as though a bomb was taped to the back. I saw weapons everywhere; wine glasses, our pepper grinder, the electric mixer—even the twist tie on the bagels looked like a mini-garrote. Patty seldom displays true homicidal tendencies, but why tempt fate with so many real and impromptu weapons close at hand?

A recent British survey revealed that 85 percent of women are put off by the kitchen habits of their men. I'd offer some snide quip like, "What are men doing in a woman's place, anyway?" but most of my future goals involve the ability to walk and the use of an attached, functioning head. Among the survey sample, 32 percent of wives were most frustrated by messes associated with their husbands' cooking, followed by 30 percent who go apeshit when they discover a fettuccini Alfredo-caked pan in the sink. Presumably, those men who are messy both *while* cooking and *after* risk summary execution. I can't imagine these numbers differ much here in America. I can certainly vouch that, with no statistical margin of error, we've realized a solid hundred percent on these measures in our home.

Don't get me wrong. I don't regard cooking or clean-up as Patty's eminent domain. I love the former and despise the latter. But if I make the mess, I'm also on the hook for cleaning up, or at least for discarding all cooking implements and replacing them with new clones. Where we don't see eye to eye, though, is in the timing and thoroughness of a dinner clean-up. To me, dishes must be addressed the next time you can't find a suitable substitute (a medium-sized vase can in fact double as a cereal bowl, drinking glass, or juice pitcher). To Patty, the restoration of this space must commence after the last bite of food enters the mouth but before it is swallowed. If I take a spoon from the drawer to stir a dish of food in the microwave, and leave the room for less than a minute, I'll find that same spoon rinsed and in the dishwasher when I return to administer a second stir.

What's more, my idea of clean—dishes washed and left to dry on a towel next to the sink—doesn't gel with hers, which is akin to sandblasting and buffing all surfaces so completely a research team bearing all manner of detection tools would swear no cooking had ever happened. If you're aware of an unsolved mystery in which someone vanished off the face of the earth, do a quick six-degrees-of-separation exercise to see if any connections lead back to Patty. She could blow someone's head off and, by the time the cops came around, even luminol wouldn't betray what happened.

I'll be the first to admit that I'm a bit of a slob. I'm sure my wife, my ex-wife, and my mother would happily second the motion and share favorite horror stories. Between them, they have more than four exasperated decades' experience picking up after me. When I first moved from home into a basement apartment, I would go weeks without lifting a finger to clean. Domestic chores became a priority only when (a) my mother was planning to visit*, (b) no clothing items could be further recycled because of armpit stains, primal odors, or skid marks (handy for making sure I didn't put underwear on backwards), (c) lichen was forming amid the dishes in the sink, or (d) the detritus was so deep I could no longer find the TV remote. This latter meant watching *The 700 Club* from time to time, because other options would involve getting up to flip the channel, which struck me as so 70s. After a week of learning just how dreadful a sinner I was, I was left little choice but to drag out the vacuum and four yard-and-garden bags I would need to have any hope of uncovering the carpet and (with any luck) the remote control.

In those days, it was not uncommon for me to prepare two bags of store-brand spaghetti (ninety-nine cents each) with two cans of no-name tomato sauce (also ninety-nine cents each)—the remaining fifty-six dollars of my weekly food allowance devoted, obviously, to vices—and then serve myself for an entire week

---

* Mother's visits demanded a special degree of fervor—storage of questionable reading material, disposal of questionable beverages, and hiding of all dinner knives, the tips of which were horribly tarnished and charred from their use in a highly questionable activity, which we shan't dwell upon.

directly from the pot on the stove. I'd add no meat to the sauce because that would mean putting leftovers in the fridge, and would also trim three bucks from my liquor budget.

When I shared this very story with Patty, she got high-and-mighty: "What on earth made you think that because your spaghetti didn't have meat, it was okay to leave out? That food was a digusting sea of bacteria." She then went on—unencouraged, I might add—to list the varieties: salmonella, staphylococcus, E. coli. All of them sounded exotic, like things I could brag about to my friends.

"Sorry, guys, no bar-hop for me tonight. Not with this damned campylobacter raging through my system." And they'd all be awed at the image of a miniaturized but still-fierce dinosaur rooting through my vital organs.

If Patty included botulism, I would have swooned. Sure it's fatal, but it just sounds so darned cool. For my last few minutes of existence, at least I could say I was taken out by one of the biggest and baddest.

Seeing I wasn't getting the point, Patty went on to list all the ailments I might have experienced: nausea, runny stools, abdominal cramping, death. Each, except maybe death, suddenly afflicted me, as though the food had been stuck in a power nap for two and a half decades and the alarm had just gone off.

I did learn a lesson on my own, though, when I left a pot of soup on the counter over a long-weekend visit to my parents' home, and returned three days later hoping to tuck into the leftovers. When I lifted the lid, with a sudden, "What in God's . . . ?" and with a sharp gag providing the exclamation, I forever after appreciated why they call it *cream* of mushroom. As a result of that misjudgment, and my earlier decision to spend my week's food allowance on beer, I had nothing to eat the next night but a tiny mound of frostbitten peas, jazzed up with a can of Franco-American chicken gravy. You won't find this recipe in *Bon Appetit* magazine, but I have no copyright on it, so serve it to your family if you wish.

With no money for smokes, I felt grateful when I happened upon two ancient cigarettes (the brand of the previous owner, who had left months before) behind the fridge, nestled on the diagonal in a dense spider-web. I didn't even mind risking hand-to-legs combat with a spider (the simple appearance of which makes me screech like a nancy-boy), or that they were stained with something orange I convinced myself was once a sauce. As they say, desperate times call for desperate measures. These were, hands down, the most rewarding cigarettes of my life, and the anonymous citrus flavor gave them extra oomph.

There's at least a minute chance I'd be in the same apartment today were it not that my landlord was a complete Neanderthal, like yours truly, when it came to any sort of repairs. Further, he was, to use the words my mom used for me, "as lazy as they come." As a consequence, whenever I was away and weather rolled in, such as a heavy downpour with strong winds, leaves would accumulate on and clog the drain near my door. I would return to find anything in my apartment less than two inches tall completely underwater. Instead of proposing a viable solution to the problem, such as some sort of bubble grate over the drain, my landlord instead handed over an enormous supply of bath towels and permission to use the dryer. For my part, I just kept several pairs of rubber boots inside the door. I'm amazed that, in some forced evolution, I didn't grow gills.

Many times I've pictured how Patty might have fared under these conditions. Most often, I get an image of her re-packing boxes before the last is even off the moving truck.

"Don't get comfy."

Today, I'm somewhat more evolved. Years of living with Patty have taught me the path of least resistance is smoother than the rocky path of greatest agitation. I've come along enough, even, to have become a bit of a hypocrite. For example, I nag my children tirelessly about dropping their backpacks on the living room floor when they come home from school. Yet I think nothing about using our stairs as a bookshelf, our coffee table as a computer desk, and the edge of the kitchen counter as a storage area for my wallet, cell phone, three days' mail, a handful of change, and various scraps of paper culled from my pocket.

And I'm guilty, over and over, of forgetting to change the bathroom garbage. Just last week, the contents were piled so high that the toilet seat cover, when moved a mere hair, triggered an avalanche of empty rolls, shaving cartridges, tissue, and a magazine with a dead fly on it. But at least I don't leave unrefrigerated leftovers with cream-based soups in them on the stove anymore. You see, even I can learn.

This budding hypocrisy hasn't come without consequences. During my first marriage, I once picked a fight with my then-wife over the distribution of chores, using the ages-old and utterly dim argument, "I work outside the home, and you work in the home, so you should keep the house clean." Taking such provocative digs is never a good idea, but is especially ill advised when (a) you're by far the worst offender, (b) the person is already cleaning when you decide to have your little talk, and (c) you emphasize your point, and your own stupidity, by mimicking your spouse's agitated tone. My ex, who was washing dishes when I launched my brainless attack, felt compelled to retort by snaking her hand out of the soapy water and slapping me across the face. Stunned, I didn't heed the warning blow and, before I could react, I received a second, more substantial thwap across my cheek.

"Why did you hit me? I thought we said we would never hit each other."

"Well, I didn't *want* to hit you, but you were really pissing me off."

"Then why did you hit me twice?"

"I thought I missed the first time."

I still can't understand why this sounded so logical to me.

In spite of my reluctant evolution, borne in part from sudden blows to the noggin, I do think some get carried away. Case in point: our neighbors may devote an entire Saturday to scouring their home from top to bottom, and yet, when Patty visits, they still apologize for the state of their home. For some reason, Patty strikes more fear into them than she does into me—and I'm usually plenty scared.

"Please, Patty, oh please, for the love of God, ignore this disaster! We weren't expecting you."

"Oh, don't be silly. It's fine. Have you seen *my* house?" They have, and that's exactly their point.

And then there's Cleaning Lady Day. Patty regards this festival of the domestic, with encores every other Thursday, with such anticipation and reverence it should be a national holiday. What's more, it would be celebrated with helium balloons, brilliant streamers, tumbling clowns, and days off work (one of which would be devoted to cleaning up all the party favors).

I could perhaps share some of this excitement—since, in spite of my track record, I enjoy our clean home, for the twenty minutes it stays that way—were it not for the gyrations and ministrations that precede it. You see, before the cleaning ladies do their thing on Thursday, everyone in our home must first participate in Wednesday's exhaustive exercise of getting our house "cleaning-lady ready." From where I sit, this involves doing in advance much of what we're paying others to do. From where Patty runs around putting everything in order, this is a natural step toward ensuring our helpers do a thorough job. This argument I cannot win.

One argument I will even *make* for Patty is that nobody makes things easier for her. We're the worst housemates for someone of her disposition. Consider laundry. Patty pretty much does it all (as do 68 percent of women, according to a 2007 Gallup poll), and she does it alarmingly often. I tried to help, but after underwire bras emerged from the dryer so reconfigured the only way Patty could ever wear them again would be with breasts at Picasso-esque right angles to her ribcage, I was excused—forbidden, really—from touching her clothes again.

Fortunately, I'm not the only one who daily incurs her wrath.

"Kids!" They're already on their way, believe me, but Patty wants to be sure of their speedy arrival. "Kids! Kids!"

"Y . . . yes, Mother?"

"You're making me absolutely crazy." She actually says "absolutely" as four words. Ab. So. Lute. Ly. "Why are there *clean* clothes in the *dirty* laundry?" She's using that special voice only mothers can master, the one that's like screaming in your face but with little change in tone.

"They're not clean . . . we swear." It took me a while to catch on, but I've learned that when a kid says, "I swear," about anything, he's really saying, "I'm lying through my teeth." If the kids are speaking true in this instance, they've each had four complete changes of clothes daily for half a week running. I can almost believe this. But a better guess is that when we forced them to clean their rooms, various items sitting on the floor as runners-up to the clothing items actually chosen went right into the hamper.

"You're sure?"

"We swear." They think they have her. They don't.

Whereupon Patty, with a smug grin the kids dare not share,

produces more than one clean shirt, as neatly folded as when first tossed in the hamper.

Patty's not alone in her frustration. The bees in my bonnet include finding the ingredients for a long-ago-consumed sandwich (turkey, cheese, mayo) left open to the elements—and to the ants—and turning off lights left on through every square inch of our house, even though everyone has gathered in a single room lit only by candles.

So, as you can see, I'm not the neatest guy, and change has been slow and bumpy. The bathroom garbage is again a towering menace. Still, a carrot dangles before me here. A recent study published in the *American Journal of Public Health* points out a significant association between a husband's participation in domestic chores and his wife's emotional well-being. It's hard to argue with health—the shoring up of hers and the preservation of mine. *Parenting* magazine ups the ante with their own poll, which showed that 15 percent of women are not only happy, but physically turned on when their partner shares the load. Bingo!

Roll out the vacuum and toss me the Windex, honey—when we're cleaning-lady ready, I'll be ready *for you*.

Things Weigh Heavily on Me . . . All Over Me

It's morning, I'm in the shower, and all my thoughts scream for breakfast. No, not a continental breakfast, which is no meal at all, but a diabolical marketing ploy by second-rate hotels to sell the myth of a hearty repast when all that's up for grabs is a bullshit snack. A mini muffin, half a grapefruit, and cup of low-fat yogurt may be just the ticket for girls, or for guys who eat like girls—you know, the ones who pick delicate bits off a muffin and then lick each finger in turn, instead of jamming at least half into their mouths in a single bite. Such sparse offerings won't get it done for this big boy.

No, what I want—what I'm lusting over—is a bacon-ham-sausage-four-egg-and-cheese skillet adrift in a sea of salty butter. And throw in some corned-beef hash on the side. In my dreams the night before, I've chased off sugar-plum fairies with a machete through a forest of fries in a spirited quest for the best burger the world has ever known. All I've eaten, though, is great gobs of stale air.

When I wake, I flip the sheets off my wife, hoping against hope I'll come face to face with a juicy, roasted turkey leg, like in the old cartoons. I'm tempted to lick her arm once, just to be sure. I don't. Just about everything in the world tastes like chicken, but Patty, I am sure, does not. This sudden nude moment turns out to be unexpected and not entirely welcome. Patty grumbles, "Stop that," and flips over in a huff.

So I hop under the streaming water and daydream about foods so utterly devoid of nutrition my arteries contemplate a sudden pre-emptive strike.

And then, out of nowhere, I have a come-to-Jesus moment. I am given a sign, an epiphany about the error of my ways and my last hope for redemption. It arrives not with a bang, like a thrashing, twitching cardiac arrest, nor with a whimper, but as a barely perceptible *ching*! As I lather, a lone nickel tumbles out of my ass, spins twice on the floor of the shower stall, and then settles.

"What the . . . ?" I look down, incredulous. I wait for a moment to see if I'm becoming a golden goose or a one-armed bandit, but the rain of coins has stopped at one.

I wrap a huge bath sheet around me—barely—and walk into the bedroom.

"Honey, I think I need to drop a few pounds. Get this—money just fell out of my ass."

"That's awesome, dear." She yawns, stretches, looks thoughtful for a moment, then adds in a hopeful tone, "Did you by any chance find our missing keys?"

Funny. I didn't laugh at that, nor did I guffaw when she suggested I replant the nickel to see if I might sprout a money tree.

You see, women have little sympathy for men who complain about their weight. I believe this desensitization is both evolutionary—a tit-for-tat thing—and fair. A recent study showed that 56 percent of women regard weight as their greatest worry, well ahead of cancer, which scored only 23 percent. Some may even hope for cancer, just so it can help ravage them into a size two. Men should heed these statistics, but instead they throw napalm atop an already raging fire. Women grow weary of hearing endless party banter about their pizza-dough asses and thunder thighs from drunken husbands sporting hard-wired empathy bellies.

"She sure as shit isn't the girl I married, I'll tell you that. When we first met, she ate nothing but water, and not much of that, either. Now look at her. If I don't hide the corn dogs in the bottom of the freezer, she'll gorge until she bursts."

I look at this particular husband with a mixture of horror and awe. How can a man stand around with his shirt off, hairy gut obscuring the entire band of his clearly—and I mean a little too clearly—undersized swim trunks, and offer up a gem like, "Have you seen my wife's tits lately?" (a somewhat loaded question), while forcing a fifth deviled egg into his mouth? Don't we have mirrors in America? And electric chairs?

These same guys show solidarity with their life partners by wolfing down two-thirds of an Angus cow and a football-sized spud obscured by full-fat sour cream while, across the table, their wives pick at half a tiny chicken breast and six green beans, all boiled. All the while, they're thinking they'll soon be gifted with a stone-cold hottie upon which they can stretch their ample bulk. Yuck.

So here I find myself, five more cents to my name but infinitely wealthier in what I perceive to be newfound wisdom. In case you didn't catch it, the key word here is "perceive."

"That's it," I say. "I can't go on like this a moment longer. We're going on a diet."

"*We* are? How did I become part of this? I'm not the one sporting an upright Hoover Wind Tunnel for an ass."

"I just think it's time for us to make a change, to start with a clean slate. Besides, don't you want to lose . . ."

The look on Patty's face says, "Say one more fucking word, I double-dog dare you."

"What I meant to say was . . ."

An apparition of my father appears, like a diminutive Obi Wan Kenobi with a less-satin, non-British voice. "Careful, son. You're crossing into dark territory here. Remember, a woman is like a caged badger. Sure, she's cute—hell, she's adorable—but provoke her and she'll growl, and snarl, and come at you with extreme prejudice. All razor claws and teeth and unrestrained fury. Caress that fragile psyche—her psyche, Brian, not her leg—and for the love of God, be careful. Better to . . . oh, wait, your mother's calling. Gotta run."

And just like that, I'm alone with my badger. And then it comes to me.

"All I'm saying is that I want to spend a long, long life with you, shopping for expensive clothes and hearing all about your day, and if we commit ourselves to getting fit—I mean fitter, 'cause you look just awesome—just look at you—then I can count on a great many more of those days."

Was that a low growl? Dear God, did she just sniff the air? My fight-or-flight mechanism screams, "Flee! Flee!" But, just like that, the malice disappears, and I'm mostly safe. For now.

"Okay, honey. Let's talk about this later," Patty replies. Translation: "We'll never speak of this again." Some issues, when pressed, beg for hostility. I'm given this one chance to back down and walk away. So I do.

I have become a master of shifting illusions, a jiggling enigma in size forty slacks. When I met Patty nine years ago, I weighed 192 pounds, stretched evenly over a six-foot-plus frame. I didn't have a six-pack—never have, never will—but I wasn't sporting a keg either. I exercised when I could, watched what I ate, and none of my clothes had labels featuring an XL with a number in front. Eight years and about sixty pounds later, I feel like I sold Patty a three-stone bill of goods—no exchanges, no returns. Sure, Patty's weight has fluctuated a little over this time, but what's remarkable with her is how joyously any extra pounds distribute themselves—who on God's green earth will complain about breasts that morph, as if by magic, from a regular C to a large D?

I recently read the results of a 2007 study conducted by the Obesity Society, an organization that, by its name, should certainly elect me to its board of directors. They found that, on average, women gain twenty-four pounds, and men, thirty, during the first five years of marriage. I've simply and gloriously carried this trend out for several more years. At this rate, I'll be into *Guinness* (the book, not the beer) by the time I score a senior's discount at Old Country Buffet.

Part of my problem is that I'm a classic yo-yo dieter. Here's the rub: I suck at using a Yo-Yo. The wooden piece drops, comes back about three inches, falls dejectedly, and then spins a couple of times in pathetic death throes before stopping completely—a nearly perfect metaphor for my attempts to regulate my weight. In one photograph, I look like one of those emaciated kids in Africa to whom my heart goes out but my money does not. In the next, I look like Orson Welles before he ate himself into the afterlife. As I review my photographic history, I realize I've been Jack Spratt, his wife, and Sybil all rolled into one.

In 1991, when I ran my first and only marathon, I weighed 155 pounds and obsessed about everything that crossed my lips. Receiving a birthday card from my brother with a giant pig diving with an open maw into an equally giant cake provided the impetus for this temporary change in ways. Once, when the only food available was pizza, I stripped the slice of everything but sauce, chewed the pieces enough to drain them of flavor, and then spit the now-vile paste into a napkin. Deathly afraid oils from my mouth might leach into my stomach, I stole a mouthful of Scope from my host's bathroom, and then fretted about calories from the mouthwash. Some people considered this a tad obsessive. This perception was compounded when, while dining with friends at an Italian restaurant, I summoned the waiter.

"Yes, excuse me. On your menu you don't seem to list any items that use whole wheat pasta. Is there any chance you might have a wholegrain option of some kind? Perhaps a quinoa penne, or a spelt linguine?"

"Uh . . . I don't think so, sir."

"Oh dear. Now tell me, when you cook the pasta, do you use any oil? Not just in the dish, but in the actual water you use to boil it?"

"I really don't know. I guess I could ask."

"Would you? Okay, now let's talk vegetables. I think I want this dish, but I wonder . . . the onions and peppers—are they steamed?"

At this point, he's giving me a look that says, I don't care enough, nor am I paid enough, nor could I be paid enough to make this interrogation worthwhile.

"I'm pretty sure they're sautéed, sir. No vegetables, then?"

"Unless the cook could steam them?"

On his pad, he writes "no veg," and then sigh-speaks, "Will there be anything else, sir?" There's subtext in his tone; so, while he's sounding helpful, what he's meaning is, "Why are you such a total dick?"

I'm about to ask if it would be too much bother for him to bring me a printout of the nutritional content of my desired meal when I am dissuaded by several sets of shoes kicking me on both shins, in unison and with extreme prejudice. I glance at the tables around us and notice other diners are hoping they might too be invited over to have a go. Suddenly, the whole environment has the feel of the Orient Express.

"No, that will be fine," I say, pouting. The waiter starts to walk away, presumably toward the manager's office where he will quit the restaurant business forever.

"Oh, oh, sorry . . . one more thing?" I reach into a bag under the table and produce a plastic container. "Would it be too much trouble for you to use *my* sauce?"

To my surprise, my friends looked mortified, and perhaps even homicidal; I have no idea what they look like today, as I haven't seen most of them since. Some people insist on being so damned proper.

Sure, time, experience and an occasional desire to see my feet have helped me make the most of ultra-low-fat cooking when I've felt the need. For example, I can whip together a meal of multigrain rotini in chicken broth with steamed asparagus, grape tomatoes, onions, peppers, and shrimp that most people could actually eat, and some may even feign to enjoy. Having said this, I do tend to find a fair amount of the meal tucked under the outer edges of plates; perhaps my guests are hoarding it for later? And yet fat-free anything somehow lacks the special mouth feel that comes from stuffing in a load of waffle fries with spicy chili, cheddar cheese, and sour cream.

After the Great Nickel Incident, Patty and I did stay the course for a short while. We rolled around on our inline skates, made an effort to eat one or two items each day not dripping in butter, and even joined the local gym. We went religiously the first week, sporadically through the next three, and have not crossed the threshold in four months. We pay seventy dollars a month just to keep our options open. Patty's boobs are in flux, caught between C and D. I can live with this. Patty cannot.

"I don't have any bras that fit anymore. If I wear a D, I'm swimming in it. If I wear a C, my boobs squeeze together and I spill out the top." My vote was to stick with the C.

Today, on one of those rare occasions each week when we splurge, I find myself in McDonald's. I order a Big Mac value meal, size large (no super size anymore; thanks, Morgan Spurlock, you jackass), a double hamburger, plain, from which I strip the meat and add it to the Big Mac, and a Quarter Pounder with Cheese (no pickle, extra onion). I wash it down with a Diet Coke, for which I compliment myself on my restraint. For me, it would seem, there are no happy mediums.

Pets—A Cautionary Tale

I promised myself—in writing—I would never, ever, share memories about a favorite pet. It's right there in my notebook. Amid the uncertain and as-yet-unformed writing ideas, like "penis caught in zipper . . . Mom?" and "snowbank in kitchen as practical joke . . . *bad* idea," it's the lone absolute. Screaming off the paper in insistent block letters with multiple solid underlines is a crystal-clear instruction: "RESIST THE URGE . . . NO PET PROSE!!!"

Here's a little experiment to help you understand why. Indulge me. Select a favorite humorous memoir. Now, starting at page one, count the pages until the author introduces a beloved yet quirky dog or neurotic cat. Nine times out of ten, you won't be fifty pages in before you're there. With gay men, it's almost always a chihuahua, bichon frisé, or Yorkshire terrier—a rat-like micro-pooch they can schlep from boutique hotel to boutique hotel in a fashionable and absurdly expensive lambskin shoulder bag (animals within animals . . . it's as cute as turducken). I'm not homophobic—not at all—but come on, guys, man up! Usually, it's a dog Partner One wanted and Partner Two did not, but Partner Two, with weakened resolve, finally bought for Partner One as a reluctant gift soon neither could live without. Puke.

With single or divorced women, it's the cats whose shortcomings provide handy metaphors for the men no longer in their lives, and whose strengths stand out in comic contrast to the men no longer in their lives. Something like, "At last I could rub a furry tummy and be rewarded with a loving purr, instead of incessant whining about his unmet needs." Again, puke. Ladies, did you know male cats have tiny penises that cause the female to yowl in pain upon withdrawal—not from size (better to go with a stallion, about eighteen inches), but because of sharp, backward-facing spines? Not so glamorous now, are they?

So why do I find myself doing this? Why am I now toking on this opium of the masses? Think of it as a cautionary tale, a one-time public service. Like the service I provide when someone sends me a holiday card I just know includes a family photo with a yellow lab front-and-center, usually bearing a set of felt antlers supporting Christmas tree ornaments. Just adorable. Ditto when someone mails a birth announcement in which the "baby" is the new puppy she bought because she's too damned lazy to have unprotected sex and shit out a real child. I aggressively scribble, "Return to Sender; Addressee Moved—Antarctica," pop it back in my mailbox, and raise the flag. To all of like mind, you're welcome.

When I was a teenager, our family acquired not one, but two dogs, both beagles. Echo was the more boisterous of the two. He was okay with being stroked, but if you tried to inch him off your bed—or, as far as he was concerned, *his* bed— he would bare his teeth and emit a low growl. This early warning system provided a handy excuse for never making my bed, so I didn't push the issue . . . or the dog. Echo also did the most adorable thing—he'd saunter in while my brother and I were watching television, squat like a center lineman ready to snap a football, and instead snap off a tightly coiled pile on the carpet before us. He'd then look at us, as if to say, "Not bad, huh? And get this—I was just outside."

We would pull our shirts up over our faces, like bank robbers, and pretend this grotesque indecency hadn't just gone down before our eyes. If we tilted our heads just so, we could ease the offending pyramid out of our range of vision, so that if my mother walked in we could both pretend we hadn't noticed. When Echo returned moments later, not to apologize ("Sorry, guys, I guess that was disgusting"), but to consume the evidence, we decided there was nothing on television we'd ever want to see again, and went outside.

Minnie was a very timid animal. She kept a wary distance from us for many months, and never barked—not once—until our family taught her to. What possesses people to cajole a dog into begging for food because it seems just so cute, and then to chide the same animal when, day and night, it won't shut the hell up?

"So, today at school . . ."

Barkbarkbarkbarkbark.

"I was in gym, and . . ."

Barkbarkbarkbarkbark.

"I was in gym, and . . . go away, Minnie."

Barkbarkbarkbarkbark.

"Minnie, stop!"

Barkbarkbarkbarkbark. . . .

"Here, have my porterhouse."

More than once as a grownup, I arrived home with a new pet, in the hopes that, against all odds, this time would be different. Our first kitten, aptly named Diablo, lasted all of one week before we begged his original owner to take him back. Comatose all day, he would suddenly burst into life at night, like the revered Transylvanian count. He'd creep into the kids' rooms, skulk under their sheets, and bite their toes so hard, and so often, that paroxysms of hysteria would accompany the mere knowledge the kitten was on the same floor, let alone in the same room. Adios, Diablo!

Our next and final foray began when I adopted a kitten from the local animal shelter. Smokey had numerous charms—for example, he's the only cat I've ever known to accompany his owners on walks, like a dog—but over time it became apparent we would need to send either Smokey or Patty packing. Like Lyle Lovett and Julia Roberts, some pairings are just wrong and destined to end badly.

Patty could overlook some of the cat's quirks, like a tendency to take naps in the Christmas tree, which resulted in countless minor injuries to our home's human occupants, who would hobble into the kitchen, bleeding, for removal of broken glass ornaments. She mostly held her tongue when Smokey shed so much hair on one of the kid's bunk beds you could fashion a new cat from the sloughings of the current one. The final straw came when Smokey decided that, no longer content to limit himself to the claustrophobic confines of his pristine litter box, he would use everything in our house—and I mean everything—as his personal urinal.

"Brian, come here, now, hurry, now. Oh, this is so gross. I'm really going to be sick."

Patty stands in the kitchen with a package of rotini in one hand and her other hand held up in front of her. She looks ready to perform a double self-amputation. Her hands, at least a foot apart, are connected by a thick, sinuous strand of yellow taffy that looks like warmed trick bubble gum. The last time I was this afraid of what would happen next was when I first watched *The Blair Witch Project*. And now a similar horror unfolds before my unbelieving eyes.

"It's cat piss. Oh, this is nasty, this is so, so nasty. Brian! Brian, there is cat piss on our food! Our *food*!"

"Oh, c'mon, honey, it's not cat piss. You're getting carried away. Do you really think the cat would piss on our food?"

She looks at her hands, and then at me, furious. "Yes, Brian. *Yes I do*."

"It's not piss." I think if I say it enough times, I'll wish this to life.

"Then *what* is it? Okay, smart guy, what is all over my hands? Oh, this is just great!"

"I don't know . . ." I'm really reaching here. "Orange juice?"

She comes at me, all fingers pointed at my face. Does she think she's going to strangle me—or that I'll even let her near me—with those filthy hands?

"Try it!" I'm *not* trying it. "Go ahead and taste it and tell me this tar that's all over me is orange juice!" Okay, okay, you win—it's cat piss.

Even if it isn't, I'm not going to sample some mysterious goo that found its way into our pantry, especially goo of a piss-like hue. We go out for dinner that night, and the next. And the next. We spend roughly a half-million dollars at the supermarket to replace every food item in our home with a urine-free clone. Even food on the top shelves is replaced, because it may have been exposed to airborne piss vapor. We use so much disinfectant in our pantry that for days no one can enter; it's our own private Chernobyl. Patty is taking no chances.

Things were bad enough when Smokey was obvious about his intent, such as every time he ambled slowly behind our family room chair, emerging a moment later with a self-satisfied post-BM look on his face. The only thing missing was a rolled up issue of *Cat Fancy* tucked up under one leg. We thought we were solving his pattern—poop on the carpet in hidden locations, pee on anything we might have hoped to eat, nothing in the litter box—but we hadn't even scratched the surface. We found feces in closets, on shelves, in the garden, and on the basement stairs. We couldn't even get close to some clothing, pillows, oatmeal packets, bags of potatoes, or sleeping bags—all bore the distinctive aroma of Smokey's Peeing Paradise. "What the . . ." became our new favorite sentence starter.

The final straw came one holiday season, as we prepared to hang our outdoor Christmas decorations. I pried the lid off a large, tightly sealed tub in which we stored all our hopelessly tangled strands of lights, and came face-to-face with an honest-to-God mystery. The wires and bulbs looked as though they were trapped in amber, like petrified insects from before the dawn of man. As I leaned in for a closer look, something else timeless and evil assailed my nostrils—cat urine, in amounts that, in spite of my horror, inspired a form of twisted awe. To this day, we haven't the faintest idea how an average-sized cat could remove the lid, do his business for what had to be a full half-hour, and then reseal the works to be discovered later, a terrible biohazard surprise. All of this within five feet of a clean litter box.

When I returned Smokey to the animal shelter a day or two later, I carried with me loads of shame, his mobile carrier, a bag of unopened cat food, and an immutable truth—I must never again own a pet. They can't live with me, I can't live with them and, as long as they're around, none of us can live with Patty. Smokey was snatched up by an older couple the next day; I thought of this as a new chance for him. As I filled out the return form, I looked at the box that queried, "Reason for return?" I thought for a moment, and wrote, "Strong allergic reaction." It's not a full truth, but it's only half of a lie.

A Day in the Life

Tuesday

6:30 a.m.I wake up. I'm still alive. Good—at least we got that out of the way. I've awakened successfully for 15,961 days and counting, unless you count that one business trip in Orlando when my morning didn't start until late-afternoon, and then with a record-setting ten-yard dash to the hotel bathroom sink. No time to dwell on vomit stories; we have a big day ahead!

6:35 a.m.I scratch myself. I pee (yes, I am in the bathroom by this point). I jump into the shower where, with just a hint of shame and a lot of naughty glee, I pee again, and then get out to dress. I choose the same jeans, T-shirt, and sweatshirt I had planned to wear to the White Sox–Blue Jays game that was postponed by rain the night before. I do a sniff-check on both armpits; not great, but they'll pass. I'll be outside for most of the day, and in a crowd big enough to keep me ambiguous in my aroma.

6:50 a.m.I drive Patty to the high school where she teaches art. I need the car today, because I am pulling the kids from school—in just the second week—to catch the make-up game, now the first tilt in a split doubleheader. Any small guilt I might otherwise feel about robbing young minds of education is assuaged by the knowledge a C-note—already spent—isn't going entirely to waste.

7:00 a.m.I sit at the computer and, for ninety minutes, read one online article after another about how the White Sox–Blue Jays game was rained out the night before. Sports news, however inane, is my crack cocaine.

8:30 a.m................................. I wake the kids, who are of course pricks about my doing so, even though they've reveled in an extra hour or two of dream time. I field obvious questions about the weather (it's sunny—can't they just open the door and find out for themselves?) and answer sarcastically that in spite of my secret fetish for stealing and hoarding kids' favorite clothes, I haven't the faintest idea, and even less interest, where their white V-neck T-shirt or hooded sweatshirt could be. "No, I didn't hide your shoes." "No, I don't know if Mom did laundry last night." "No, I'm not washing that before we go." I wait for an equally sarcastic response. None comes; lucky them.

9:30 a.m.We drive to the Aurora train station, roughly an hour from the city. En route, I briefly entertain the first of what are sure to be thousands of perplexing and inane questions from Connor, our youngest son: "Are we going to leave the car when we take the train into the city?" I start to answer, "No, we're going to heave it on the roof of . . ." Oh, never mind.

At the station, as always, there's not a single parking space. Some commuters have jammed their cars into gaps where there are no official spaces, but I'm too much of a coward to take this chance. We move on to the casino three blocks away and park in their garage. Two bucks for the entire day, a real bargain compared to the twenty-two dollars we paid for a parking pass for last night's game—money we have now pissed away, because:

(a) I won't drive to the park, which sits in a somewhat seedy neighborhood in which I'm certain to become hopelessly lost and even more hopelessly vulnerable, and

(b) I will never remember to redeem the pass for its value in Comiskey Cash, which I imagine might buy roughly half of a logo-adorned golf towel.

We walk to the train station.

10:00 a.m.I order four tickets—one adult, three students—return, Chicago Union Station. I answer, "Yes, by 'return' I mean both to and from Chicago," and "Yes, by 'students' I mean high school age or younger," and "Yes, I think they have their student IDs, would you like to see them?" For a second, I wonder if Connor has morphed into a middle-aged African-American woman and stolen into the booth for the express purpose of fraying my last nerve. He's standing right next to me, looking up. "What?"

10:15 a.m.We arrive on the train platform. I light a cigar and puff madly to ensure I'll have enough angst-soothing nicotine in my bloodstream for the eighty-five-minute train trip; I will do the same seconds after I arrive in Chicago to make sure I'm covered off for the rest of the jaunt to the park. Sated for now, I extinguish the half-smoked cigar.

A wash of cool dread pours over me as an announcement is made that the "equipment" (I presume they mean "train," but apparently hearing the straight truth may be too painful for some of us) will be held up first twenty-six minutes, then twenty-eight, and then indefinitely (uh-oh . . . better dig out the parking pass).

In transportation parlance, "indefinitely" translates roughly into "you're fucked." I kill time first by imagining that someone on my burgeoning shit list had jumped in front of said train, and then by eavesdropping on others' conversations about unfiltered cigarettes. A seed is planted, so I relight my cigar; we could be here a while.

10:50 a.m..T h e train finally departs, thirty-five minutes late, and lumbers toward the city. I flip through a female author's memoir, skipping over discussions of shoes, shopping, and the merits of being sistas, all of which are entirely lost on me. I pause only when I get to the faintly promising part about her first experience touching a penis. I hope things will get spicy—and by this I mean pornographic—but women never describe these things in ways guys relish, so I close the book, bored. I contemplate whether or not to wake my daughter to warn her the zipper on her jeans is wide open. When I do, she informs me it's broken, and that she wears all of her jeans that way. Huh.

12:15 p.m.Our train arrives in Chicago. On foot, we make the five- or six-block trek to the subway, stopping only for me to light and relight my cigar several times, much to the delight of my hungry children. We board the 95/Ryan Red Line train to the Sox/35th stop. I keep what I deem a safe distance from a homeless person who somehow looks both asleep and angry.

12:45 p.m...................................We arrive at the park and present our tickets. We board the escalator for the nosebleed section, where, if you stayed long enough, you might gain both vertigo and enhanced sports performance. Halfway to the summit, I ask a disinterested usher bearing a sign, "500 level closed," what that means, since our tickets clearly say "Section 527, Row 4, Seats 1–5." He grunts, almost unintelligibly, "Outfield." We search for another usher. We rejoice when a park employee who has made the evolutionary leap says, "Sit where you want." We choose seats in the 100 level behind home plate, 23 rows from the field. Our luck is changing; this may well be a magical day.

12:55 p.m. At the concession stand, I order six hotdogs (five Kosher—two for me, two for PJ, one for Connor—and one regular for Kelly), four small bags of Lay's Chips, and four lemonades. The attendant asks, "Pink lemonade?" I'm tempted to ask, as I always am, how often people have a problem with the hue of their lemonade. Had I wanted a Coke, would I need to specify a *russet* Coke? The game's about to start, so I just fork over the $45.00 in *green* money and head to the condiments station.

1:00 p.m. The ketchup comes out fast. I like a whiff of ketchup. I now have a deep, unmanageable crimson mound—a hot dog crime scene. The only consolation is that the viscous liquid starts to just barely reconstitute a very stale bun. I try to tease onions out of a grinder with a crank handle a fellow attendee has warned me is broken. I try anyway, presuming he just didn't do it right. The handle comes off in my hand. I then agree it may in fact be broken. I stare at it for a full thirty seconds, lost. Mumbling something about living dangerously, I then employ a relish packet to scoop some sickly-looking onions from the tray beneath the grinder and atop my hot dog.

1:05 p.m. The game begins. After a dicey first half-inning—two Jays left on base—there's still no score. My team comes to bat. I yell, "Come on" to our leadoff hitter. The next batter hears me shout, "Nail that ball." When I scream, "We need a home run," toward the third man up, some baseball expert behind me says to his friend, in the most thinly veiled attempt to tell me to shut the fuck up, "I have to think hearing their names called when the ball is headed toward them is just distracting and annoying." His sage friend replies, "Nah, they learn to tune that shit out." I am awed and humbled by this living, breathing book-on-CD excerpt from Chapter One of *Baseball Psychology for Dummies*. For the rest of the day, I will try to keep "that shit" to myself.

2:45 p.m. .... Things are not going well, and I'm struggling to keep that shit to myself. By the bottom of the sixth, the Sox have managed only a single hit to the Jays' five. At home, I would now be storming in circles around the main floor of our house, inventing new and startling profanities because the standard ones wouldn't be vile enough. Since I'm in public with other irresponsible parents and their now-undereducated brood, I just sit there, arms crossed, with a look on my face some would describe as seething, and others might call pouting. The kids ask if they can buy long, single strands of licorice at $1.50 a pop; I just pass over my wallet and hope they'll bring it back.

4:00 p.m. The atrocity is over. Jays win 3–1. My six-game unbeaten streak while attending Sox games has come to a tragic end. I tell the kids this, thinking they will at least offer, "Sorry, Dad," and at best promise to behave like the von Trapp children for the balance of our outing. They do neither.

As we pass a Cubs fan in Cubs garb on the ramp leaving the park, I am tempted to commit homicide by flipping him over the side to the pavement below. Wearing the cross-city rival's colors in our house is akin to encouraging your dog to crap on the neighbor's lawn in plain view of the owners sitting on the porch. If I wore black-and-white to Wrigley Field, I'd expect a similar gesture.

I appreciate all the other kindred spirits who threaten this jerk-off, until more than one calls him a faggot, over and over, which makes me (and any gay fans, I am sure) acutely uncomfortable. The day has slipped from bad to worse, and I begin to anticipate even more dire fates, like getting to the L to find out the "equipment" is indefinitely on the fritz. I vow to myself that for the rest of this day, no matter what happens, I will not smile.

4:15 pm..On the L back to the Loop, I smile. Next to a woman wearing a pink Sox sweatshirt, which annoys me—just as there's no crying in baseball, there should also never be feminine colors or rhinestone logos, *ever*—a Toronto fan wears a blue shirt with a smiling bird on front. It announces, "I love my BJs." I comment, "I can't argue with that."

5:10 p.m.McDonald's at Union Station. We order food we will need to devour whole—no time for luxuries like chewing—if we hope to catch the 5:26 p.m. train back to Aurora. As we dole out our order, we happen upon an extra double cheeseburger. Connor asks, "Why would they give us an extra cheeseburger?" I treat the question as rhetorical, because any answer would be affording the question too much legitimacy and would just lead to another. We plow through the food like we're the Donner Party, and hoof it just in time to catch our train.

6:15 p.m. .... We arrive in Aurora. While walking to the casino parking lot to retrieve our car, PJ and Kelly sprint across an intersection when a light turns yellow; Connor and I are trapped until the next green. We watch as first PJ, then Kelly, disappear into the distance. I keep thinking, as their heads grow smaller and smaller, that they'll stop soon, but they just keep going. I contemplate what I want to yell at them when I catch up. The terms "rude," "asshole-ish," and "so-help-me-god-we're-never-doing-this-again" come to mind, but when we finally do rejoin them I manage only a limp, "Thanks for waiting."

7:11 p.m.We've been home for forty-five minutes, and the second game of the split doubleheader with the Jays is starting. I have just filled a sixty-four-ounce thermal mug with nine ounces of whisky, twenty-four ounces of Diet Coke, and (I guess) thirty-one ounces of ice. I'm crabby. Patty has informed me my friend Chris, from Toronto, has left two provocative and mocking messages—just as he has, religiously, each of the last six times in a row the Jays have beaten the Sox. I tell her I'm not calling until after the second game, when I can throw our impending and glorious victory back in his face.

8:15 p.m.Fifth inning. Jays 5, Sox 2. Chris calls again. I don't answer.

9:30 p.m.Seventh inning. Jays 6, Sox 2. Chris calls again. I bark, "Don't you answer that phone!" I tell Patty that Chris is the biggest asshole of all time, even worse than Hitler, Mussolini, and all Cubs fans combined, and that if he tries to reach me one more time, I will never speak to him again. I mean it.

9:40 p.m.Eighth inning. Jays 7, Sox 2. Patty tells me that if I don't stop identifying each of the players, in turn, by a different derogatory name for a female body part, she won't let me watch any more games. I'm tempted to come back with, "And you're going to stop me?" but her look tells me "Yes. Yes, I am." I call Chris and take my lumps.

11:15 p.m.The game is long over (Jays 8, Sox 2), as is my bottle of whisky and my belief I will ever again watch baseball. I've gone off on a ten-minute tangent with Kelly and Patty about how women don't know what men find beautiful in women—you're all puppets for the cosmetic industry, yadda, yadda, yadda—and that Debra Messing most certainly is not beautiful, but just a Lucille Ball clone who should wear a bra once in a while. I don't mean it; she only *acts* like Lucille Ball.

Patty suggests perhaps I'm overwrought (translation: Stop talking like a drunk in front of the kids) and that I should stop weeping and call it a day. In bed, sleep comes within nanoseconds. I dream of a train that works, heading toward a city I've come to love, and arriving at my favorite team's home just in time to see them recapture their rightful place on baseball's throne.

Tim Treadwell, We Hardly Knew Ye

My most recent longing for the great outdoors was triggered by the film *Grizzly Man*, the delightful comedy about Timothy Treadwell, whose none-too-endearing habit of nicknaming bears Booble, Squiggle, and Rowdy left them no choice but to rip him limb-from-limb and eat him. As he cooed, "Who's a big bear? Who's a big bear?" in effeminate baby-speak, I longed for the beast to answer by knocking his yammering head into the bushes. What self-respecting grizzly (or film buff) wants to listen to that? Tim, there's a reason bears choose to live hundreds of miles away from the reach of humankind, and I'm pretty sure you're it. Who's a big dead dummy? Who's a big dead dummy?

The cinematography of Alaska's soaring mountains, crystal lakes, and rugged, unspoiled terrain is so striking I can almost drown out the puerile observation, "Oh my gosh! The bear, Miss Chocolate, has left me her poop! It's her crap! It was just in her butt and it's still warm! This is a gift from Miss Chocolate!" Now, don't get me wrong—I enjoy a room-clearing fart as much as the next guy and, like most men, I find in-depth conversations about scat in its many shapes, textures, and aromas to be both hilarious and timeless. But to call it a *gift*?

What I couldn't get past, after ninety minutes of hoping—okay, praying—for horrible harm to befall this antagonist, was director

Werner Herzog's decision to exclude the tape of Treadwell being eaten, a choice that makes the whole viewing experience feel like heavy foreplay followed not by vigorous rogering but a sucker punch directly to the face. Even my kids felt ripped off.

"What, you mean we don't get to hear him getting eaten? It's not even in the special features? Did you double-check?"

"Hey, don't look at me. I was ready."

I shouldn't mock. I wouldn't pitch camp within hundreds of miles of grizzly territory. Once, a chipmunk bounced off my tent while I was trying to nap and I screamed like Dakota Fanning before sprinting a quarter-mile through the woods. I'm not what most would call a rugged outdoorsman.

Still, I forged happy memories and learned valuable lessons while camping in my youth. I discovered that running a single digit along the canvas ceiling of a pop-up trailer during a thunderstorm rendered all waterproofing useless, and that my father did, in fact, know all of the words you couldn't say on television. And that if I was craving my parents' attention, I could get it in spades by exaggerating the wheezing from my grass allergy to such an extent (*wheeeeeee . . . uhhhh . . . wheeeeeee . . . uhhh*) that we would break camp at one in the morning and rush to the nearest hospital. Good times. These, and others, made me a lifetime fan of sleeping under the stars.

So this summer, when our neighbors invited our family to visit the private campground at which they have a lot and trailer, my head filled with romantic notions of gently chirping crickets, wholesome, hearty fire-cooked meals, and the comforting melody of wood crackling in the cool, fresh air. Patty imagined *Deliverance*.

"I'm telling you this: I will *not* shit in an outhouse." Her entire body shudders, even her hair. "It's dis-gus-ting." And so it starts. I try—and fail—to keep things light.

"When I went backpacking, I dug a hole to use as a toilet. I'd just hover over it and, when I was done, I'd fill the hole with dirt."

She looks at me like I have nine heads. They're all looking back at her, unblinking, hoping for encouragement.

"And exactly *why* would you do that?"

"What else could I do?"

"Here's an idea: Don't go."

One-third of the U.S. population visits a campground at least once in any five-year period. Few regard it with as complete disdain as Patty. We've been together nine years, and this is only our second time. The first was in an air-conditioned camper, and even that left Patty grossly underwhelmed. To her, no room service means no real vacation.

Patty starts compiling a list of demands. Flush toilets within easy walking distance. Check. Showers, also close at hand. Check. Electricity. Check. Several cans of insect repellent and sunscreen. Check. Travel-sized bottles of every toiletry known to man. Check. Giant inflatable mattress, three-hundred-thread-count sheets, body pillow, electric fan. Sigh . . . check. Directions to the closest hotel.

"And you can forget about making love. Add mace to that list."

I reach for the phone; I'm calling the whole thing off. Even I have limits—it's a campground, not a Bible retreat. I decide instead to wait until we're there, and then pester her until she gives in. It may just work. And it may not.

Just before we call an end to the first night, it starts to rain. Hard. I'm delighted. I wax poetic about how the patter of raindrops on the nylon tent roof is pure nirvana, one of life's most soothing, natural lullabies. Euphoric, I look to Patty for confirmation. She looks to her purse for her credit card, cell phone, and the list of hotels.

The kids are safely settled in The Kid's Tent, placed by me several yards away in the hope Patty might consider a little *amour*—a prospect that, while a long shot to begin with, has no chance if the kids are within earshot. Patty is the first to enter our tent. She unzips the door, crawls forward, stops, and bursts into tears. Her knee has plunged into the half-inch of water that covers the entire floor, now known as Lake Despair. Her recoil is reminiscent of a 12-gauge Remington shotgun.

"I can't stay in here. Oh my God. Oh . . . my . . . God! We are going to get so sick . . . we might even die. I can't believe you talked me into this, and everything's soaked, and there's water everywhere, Brian, everywhere! How did all this water get in here? And everything's going to totally stink, shit, shit, fuck, oh shit, my clothes are ruined, just ruined, we may as well just throw everything out. Why are you laughing? You think it's funny that we could very well die out here?"

Sorry, but I think it's fucking hilarious.

"Move out of the way. I'm sleeping in the truck."

In damage control mode, I grab a handful of beach towels, most of my clothes, and an entire roll of paper towels and mop up about half of the water. I assure Patty that since we're on the air mattress, we'll stay above the dampness. Hopeful, I suggest it's not unlike sleeping on a waterbed, and we all know for what waterbeds are revered. What I'm selling, she's not buying. But, exhausted from crying, she agrees to just settle in and leave the split-second the sun comes up.

My head hits the pillow at the precise moment the first drop of water strikes the center of my forehead. Plink! I say nothing. I pray the percussion sounded louder in my skull than it did in the tent at large. Another drop, and another. I still say nothing. I weigh the relative discomfort of suffering through Chinese water torture or discovering Patty's reaction to this latest surprise. (Bring it on, Mao.) Soon, it's moot. The water has started to fall on Patty as well.

"Oh, you have *got* to be kidding!" I wait for more fireworks, but Patty just climbs off the mattress, tells me to do the same, pulls our bed six inches further down the tent, climbs back on, and tries to go to sleep. I snuggle up to her.

"Don't! I *will* kill you." I don't. I begin a slow and moist fade to black.

As the sun rises, the mattress is flat; it seems the air had no desire to stay in a wet tent. There's little water on the floor, because our sleeping bags have done a yeoman's job of absorbing most every drop. I know the precise location of each of my major organs—kidney, liver, spleen—because all feel like they've been laid into by Mark Tyson. I need to urinate more than ever before, an emergency I address by opening the tent and peeing directly onto the spot where we will soon crawl out. Patty's still asleep, so I dodge that bullet.

When our hosts emerge from their bone-dry, warm, and spacious trailer an hour or so later, they offer a too-warm smile and ask, "So, how was your night?"

Here we go. I look for cover, or for one of the kids to employ as a human shield. Should I smash the love of my life in the back of the head with a shovel before she has a chance to open her mouth? When she came to an hour or three later, I could explain away the tennis-ball-sized bump by recalling the attack of a volleyball-sized mosquito. If I bribe the kids enough, they'll even back me up. "Yeah, Mom, the mosquito was so full of your blood he couldn't fly—we just kicked him into the woods."

But Patty surprises me. "Oh, it was just fine." I just love this woman.

Through the next day, the sun beats down without mercy, and swarms of flies beset us from all directions. Have I mentioned that Patty's no fan of flying insects? Our neighbors and our children try to improve our situation by smiting a handful of the interlopers with a flyswatter. They're winning neither the battle nor the war, and soon yellow jackets, who seem at first stunned and then just pissed when struck with the swatter, join our party. Patty just sits, silent, and sears me with the "You fucker" gaze.

I look forward to the second night in the tent the way I would relish donning a suit of raw antelope meat and running amok in a crowded lion enclosure—an activity only a little less safe than pushing Patty beyond her limits. Still, it's been a beautiful evening, so we agree tonight will be a better night. Actually, I promise it will be a better night—we hadn't agreed upon anything since our arrival. My gravestone may bear the epitaph: "He said it would be a better night. He was so wrong."

As we're setting up for a few hands of poker at the picnic table, another friend with a property in the campground calls our neighbor's cell phone. A severe thunderstorm will hit within an hour. As a special bonus, our little corner of the storm's path has been upgraded to include a tornado watch. Oh goodie.

My sons and I prove the maxim, "necessity is the mother of invention," when we grab two giant tarps, some rope and nails, and jerry-rig a sail of sorts over and around the tent. It looks obscene, like a hillbilly squatter's camp. The only things missing are a Confederate flag, a pregnant first cousin (triplets, no doubt, with flippers for arms), and a couple hundred hounds, all named Clem (Clem I, Clem II, and so on).

Our timing is perfect. We drive the last nail for Camp Redneck as all hell breaks loose. We hide in the trailer for an hour and listen as first rain, then hail, then cats, then dogs, then rain again pounds the campground, punctuated by massive peals of thunder. When the deluge subsides enough for us to make our way to the tent, we're relieved to discover the tent is mostly dry—ridiculously hot because of the lack of air flow, but dry. Patty is happy, so I snuggle in again. This time, it works.

Patty's list of demands for our next family getaway: Four-star hotel. Check. Heated pool. Check. Twenty-four-hour room service. Check. Twelve-dollar carafe of coffee. Anything you want, honey. Anything at all.

My Wife Told Me Not to Write About Sex

After I first approached Patty with my idea for a book, and threw in bold claims about large advances, abundant royalties, and foreign distribution rights—I may have even tossed in "Pulitzer" once, for effect—I found Patty in the kitchen in a quasi-orgasmic trance, twirling, daydreaming, and talking to herself in a sing-songy voice.

"Helen Hunt's going to play me in the film version, and I'm going to fancy parties, and maybe meet someone who picks up after himself . . . I bet George Clooney picks up after himself. Hey, how long have you been standing there?"

She was happy. Not only would kindred spirits the country over share in mocking my abundant shortcomings, but, if the book shot up the bestseller lists, she might even score a new car.

"You know I'm not greedy. Really, Brian, as long as when I tell my friends I can use the words 'new' and 'Mercedes'—oh, yeah, and maybe 'convertible'—you're golden."

In truth, Patty would settle for any combination of "vehicle" and "not the one we have right now." There's good reason. Every time we climb into our car there's just a one-in-five chance the ignition will catch the first time. If it does, everyone lets out this deep, collective sigh and adopts this dopey smile that says, "Oh my God, I just can't believe it." If it doesn't start, humiliation breaks over us in great, cresting waves.

It's not just that the car doesn't start—*that* we could live with. No, it both *doesn't* start and *does* emit an ear-piercing screech that causes passersby to drop packages and grab their chests in shock. Some even protectively clutch their children to their bosoms. This cycle repeats five to seven times, attracting ever-larger and increasingly hostile crowds, before the engine finally catches and we can begin therapy on each other. Our neighbors have discarded their alarm clocks; they just wait for Patty to leave for work in the morning. Sure, once a week they need to make excuses for being late, but if their workplace sits within a three-mile radius of our home, their boss knows our car and will cut them some slack.

So yes, Patty was supportive of my new venture, in that success-means-no-more-public-embarrassment-because-that-piece-of-shit-car-will-be-gone kind of way. Heady with my dreams of fame and untold fortune, and comforted my wife had agreed to stand behind my new writing career, I was in no way ready for her caveat. (It's Patty, for God's sake . . . why wasn't I ready for the caveat? Stupid, stupid, stupid!)

"Brian, do not . . . no, that's not strong enough . . . you *will* not . . . tell the whole world about our sex life." I should have seen this coming; she was none too happy when I spilled the gory details to the whole neighborhood and several of her co-workers. Even when she added, "I am *so* not kidding," and threw me the "just try me" evil eye, I just nodded stupidly, like what she had just said would make an iota of difference.

I blame my genitals and their incessant need to be heard. "Tell them," I hear from within my pants. "Tell the people. You know this zipper's just a crutch! Spread the word. Spread the seed. Divide and conquer, divide and conquer!"

"Shut up! Shut up! For just once in your post-pubescent existence, would you please shut the hell up?"

From my pants, a stony silence; was it sulking? I try to remind my little friend that *he* is nothing without *me,* but he knows better—the sum of the rest of my parts is little more than a life support system for *him.*

"*Tell* them!"

"Okay, okay, just relax."

You see, I have no choice. Patty's plea to refrain from discussing sex was, to her, a direct product of her strict Irish Catholic lineage, which dictated that any activity not utterly Draconian in nature would fling open the fiery gates of Hell. She's expected to shower after she even thinks about sex (see George Clooney, above). For me, a Protestant (Catholics may substitute "hell-bound heathen" here), and not a very good one at that, asking me to keep things clean was like beseeching a dog not to lick its own privates—a gift which, truth be told, makes me seethe with envy. I resent the lot of them, from the shittiest shih tzu to the cockiest Doberman (puns intended); they're all so freaking smug, what with their noses buried so comfortably in their balls.

I'm at a loss. If I can't write about sex, what should I expound upon—an insane phobia about flies?

We're told sex is a natural, loving interaction between two consenting adults in a healthy, committed relationship. I would add that it's also pretty damn good in the practice rounds, after you know each other's first names but before frightening words like "love" and "forever" enter the picture—but I digress. If sex is a good and righteous thing, even for some Republicans, why then must we treat it like a dirty little secret? Why not instead run through the streets screaming, "I just loooooove sex!" in your T-shirt that boldly invites, "Let me toss my junk into your backyard."

I try this tack with Patty. When I suggest I want only to provide a light-hearted glimpse at our marital bed, her head rocks violently from side to side, a turbo-charged bobblehead doll. No, no, no, no, no. Wait, was that a yes? No, no, no.

"Brian, there is just *no* way." And yet, when there's a will isn't there always a way? On the flipside, I fear my way may lead tragically to my will. Like the Australian hubby whose wife stabbed him thirty-seven times, skinned his body, cured the meat on a hook in the closet for several days, baked him, and then served him to the kids with vegetables and gravy. News reports failed to confirm whether or not the kids ate their veggies.

"What if my brothers and sisters read the book?" she asks. "What about my aunts? They don't know we have *sex*." She says the last word the way a deviant might say, "people tied up in the basement."

For once, I have a comeback. "Honey, who among that group won't skip the chapter, or burn the entire book, when they know what it's about?"

I have hit a home run—a solo shot—but my pleas find themselves in the bottom of the ninth, with two outs, and about fifteen runs to make up against an ace closer. I persist, but negotiations reach a quick impasse, one with a not-unsubtle hint of coming violence. Even my pants stay unusually quiet; they have no desire to board the express train to Bobbitville. So I'm left little choice but to say my piece on the sly. Oh well, doesn't the Lord hate a coward?

My in-laws may not read this chapter, or even a signed first edition of this book, but I suspect at least some of my children may. So, rather than heed my temptation to launch into banal descriptions of position, duration, and such (you really don't want to hear about this, anyway . . . *really*), I'll try to keep things clinical, statistical. Okay, caveats be damned—here goes.

Based on my admittedly un-Kinseylike calculations, Patty and I have done the deed 4,380 times, give or take (and, when done well, both give *and* take.) I'm not bragging, but . . . well, yeah, I guess I'm bragging.

This is no scientific measurement, mind you. I have known Patty for nine years. Years one through three were the "horizontal holiday," during which we came at each other like minks fully four or five times a day—once or twice in the morning, once right after work, and once or twice more at bedtime. Avoiding curious children became my life's great work. On more than one occasion, we found ourselves in a crumpled heap on the floor where, deep in the throes of passion, Patty didn't even note that the carpet under the bed needed vacuuming. I imagined this trend continuing well into our golden years, when the only added cautions would be to swallow great handfuls of Viagra, go easy on the artificial hips, and run the vacuum in the bedroom once a week. Alas, no.

Now, in what I've come to call "The Dark Ages" or, alternatively, "The Great Pussy Famine," we only see action four or five times a week. I know what you're thinking: if you're a guy, you see my wife as barbaric and cruel, and I'd have to agree. If you meet her, *please* tell her; she won't listen to me. You may also have noted that while Pete Rose managed only 4,256 hits in his career, I've rounded all the bases many more times than that, and I'm still on the active roster. If you're a woman, you think I'm spoiled and selfish, and that I should have taken Patty's advice and/or warning. Whatever.

I arrived at my magic number based on a very rough overall average of 1.5 times a day. The national average is just over twice a week, so ha! If you factor in the number of times I've asked, but been declined outright, usually with some let-him-down-easy comment like, "Don't be so stupid," multiply this number by ten. If you factor in the times I've been asked, and said no, hahahahahahahaha. Just stick with the original number.

My failure, as I extended the trend line o' love many years out and off the charts, was in neglecting to account for an impending menace few men can begin to appreciate, and even fewer can run fast enough to escape—menopause. I thought this was many years away, and that we would send it packing for good with a couple of maximum-strength Advil.

"Here, honey, take these. I just have to ask—did you really mean to call me an insufferable douchebag just now?"

Who even knew of such a thing as early onset menopause? How fair is that? Instead of facing down this specter in our mid-to-late fifties, when I planned to replace Patty with a twenty-five-year-old runway model (or two) anyway, menopause arrived at the door in our forties, and with all the subtlety of a roving pack of militant Jehovah's Witnesses two converts short of quota. This was no mere visit, with a weekend carry-on bag. No, the brilliant red moving van had roared up to the curb, like something out of *Maximum Overdrive*. A dark, brooding cloud formed over our home and just sat there. I was going to need something stronger than ibuprofen to vanquish this foe.

Menopause is a high-maintenance mistress, rich with frightening nuances and dangerous contradictions. Like war, but more brutal and with no prisoners spared. eHow, an online how-to guide, even has an entry for "How to not kill a spouse during menopause," which reminds women to never forget that men are simple creatures with only three emotions—happy, hungry, and horny. I don't agree with the order, but the author seems to get us.

You may think you're doing all the right things to warm your lover's heart, like remembering the anniversary not only of your wedding but also of the day you met. You continue to shower her with regular bouquets of irises, her favorite. You expect to receive a T-shirt on your birthday that exclaims "#1 Hubby," which is of course too tacky to wear but brings a tear to the eye each time you pass it over in your dresser drawer. Instead, you discover you're no hero, but instead the biggest asshole of all time—and all because she had to remind you a second time to put the empty soda cans in the recycling bin. And if she can find a shirt bearing that message, she'll make you wear it, tacky or not.

When you do convince your wife to participate in an unscheduled round of lovemaking, mostly through begging and expensive bribes, and then praise yourself for being so masterful she's left flushed and panting, you suddenly find yourself on the floor while she extinguishes a hot flash with a full bottle of Aquafina. Time to throw the trend lines out the window.

Truth be told, opening up about sex is risky—the closest analogy I can come up with is slapping a grizzly bear roundly on the snout and then traipsing off with its offspring—and these risks are not to be taken lightly. Even if your spouse isn't saying, "I swear to all that is holy that if you say one thing about what happens in our bedroom it will be a cold day in hell before you have anything new to write about," it's not easy to bare all; if you saw me naked (you won't), you'd know why.

With kids around, you can't exactly capture all the naughty nuances in your daily journal. Besides, how interesting would it be to provide a running monologue on something that, after the first few hundred times, offers little that is truly new?

June 8. Pinched left nipple—*her* left—then right, etc.
June 9. Pinched right nipple, then left, etc.
June 10. Pinched both nipples, in unison, etc., etc.

Do you see what I mean?

But I consider myself a student of the world, and in a world that includes sex, I want to talk about it, to immerse myself in it, because from great conversations come great insights. Sure,

I've read books like *Be a Madman in Bed* and *She Wants It More Than She Thinks*. These tomes promise I'll soon enjoy one-hour orgasms—a prospect that sounds at once both divine and acutely unpleasant—but then propose positions no part of my anatomy could possibly support. Countless times, I've scratched my head, turned the book in various directions, and said to myself, "Now how in God's name would that work?"

I've even rented an adult movie or two (hundred), from which I've gleaned precious little, at least in terms of carnal techniques. One exception: through trial and egregious error, I've picked up that even though the women in these films moan and buck while their partners rub their nether regions with all the speed and brute force of a power sander set on high, this approach yields little more than screams of anguish when put into actual practice.

"That's the problem with men," Patty says. "They think they can learn from those movies, but they can't because those scenes are all about what men want, not women." Sure. Next you'll be taking issue with Hooters girls. I make a note to suffer through *What Women Want* one last time, as a crash course in sensitivity training. This time, though, it will be without my mother who, each time Mel Gibson is on-screen, adopts a look of anticipation bordering on the rapturous. Creepy, just creepy. I ask Patty what film she would recommend to add spice to a marriage. Without a second's hesitation, she picks *Last of the Mohicans*. Excuse me?

"Let me get this straight. It would put you in a sexy mood if we ran around a deep forest in loincloths while I pursued you in a ravenous blood lust, only to scalp you when I finally laid hands upon you? It seems a bit extreme, but I'm game. We'll need some heavy twine, three bolts of canvas . . ." She just blinks. Clearly, she thinks I'm an idiot.

"No, idiot. What makes Daniel Day Lewis so charming is how he holds her shoulders near the waterfall and tells her, 'You stay alive. Stay alive. I will come back for you.'" Now I blink, expressionless. What on earth does that have to do with sex? I realize sex is preferable if your partner is alive, or at least pretending to be, but otherwise I can't make the connection. Besides, there had to be millions of mosquitoes in those woods, so if my hands were near Patty's shoulders, she'd be expecting me to be using them to dispatch bugs.

So, dear reader, I guess we too have reached an impasse. I had hoped to drag you, helpless, into a deep sea of debauchery, one rich with innuendo, hot chemistry, and legendary passion. Instead, thanks to Patty and the Holy See, I guess I won't write much about sex at all.

Midnight in My Garden of Pure Evil

It's official—my garden hates my stinking guts. I know, I know. You're going to argue that since plants don't have brains, and therefore lack intelligence, they can't express complex emotions like love, hate, or profound distaste for Eddie Murphy's last decade on film. Tell that to my plants. Just as sure as I am that I don't like *Daddy Day Care,* sight unseen, I somehow just know Mother Nature has her middle finger pointed squarely in my direction. Don't fall for those old Chiffon margarine commercials—where some old biddy causes a thunderstorm and teases, wryly, "It's not nice to fool Mother Nature"—she's a cold, hard bitch who has it in for me.

I should have seen it coming. Everyone has a list of strengths, and on mine landscaping sits right at the bottom, just above remembering about the toilet seat (Brian! For the Love of God—it's freezing!) and just below clearing out the fridge before forgotten veggies redefine themselves as a noxious, multicolored bisque. In the crisper, no less. Why I can cultivate whole new strains of mold indoors but crash and burn at teasing a single rose to bloom in the garden is beyond me.

Perhaps it's the male chauvinist in me standing out like a sore, non-green thumb, but I've always felt mowing was for guys, and gardens were for girls. Like cleaning the oven, scrubbing toilets, changing diapers, and doing the laundry. Oh, I'm kidding. I can do all of those things, but choose not to out of respect—Patty does them better than I do.

Still, I knew something had to be done about our flowerbeds. I'd like to say my reasons had everything to do with beautification, but my motivation was much more practical. I needed something more substantial than a dozen giant thistles to conceal the hundreds of cigar butts I'd been tossing off the front porch. I also kidded myself that an eye-catching floral display might offer an effective distraction from the result of my last failed experiment—bird-watching.

The feeders themselves were fine. If you peered through my home-office window, you might even see the odd cardinal or finch among the relentless hordes of cackling blackbirds. If I ever take up baking, I'll have my four-and-twenty many times over. The problem arose after the birds had their fill. Instead of just leaving, perhaps with a thankful chirp and a tip of the wing, the birds instead expressed appreciation by whitewashing our patio set, our gas grill, our bushes, the back step, and anyone or anything that dared step out the patio door. I tried moving the feeders further away, but soon learned birds don't mind flying a few more feet to crap all over the hand that feeds them.

Perhaps if my heart had been in the right place, and if I had taken gardening on as a labor of love, things may have played out better. But I don't think so.

Patty has a saying, "Competence is a turn-on," and I was determined that, this time, I would be over-the-top competent. She, in turn, would be so turned on she would allow me carte blanche to select items for her (okay, indirectly, for me) from the Victoria's Secret catalog. Or so I thought.

When you've never even picked up a gardening book before, and therefore know diddly about a dicey subject, it's a crapshoot. I shouldn't say I know nothing about gardening; it's just that most of what I've picked up came from *High Times* magazine, and from movies of questionable scientific accuracy.

I do know, for example, that if next to the potted ficus in your bedroom you find a giant seed pod you didn't put there, you may want to take in Letterman and a few infomercials, and opt against a good night's sleep. Also, from my DVD of *The Ruins,* which is destined to become either a classic or a wedge supporting our unsteady kitchen table, I learned that if nature is running amok outside your tent, with dead and dying folks all around, nothing eases the unbearable tension like a reach-around from your girlfriend.

Something told me none of my cinematic education was going to be of much use.

Still, with the prospect of satin-and-lace merry widows dancing in my head, I schlepped off to the Garden Center at Home Depot with two kids in tow. We picked out a few safer-looking items. We chose three hanging baskets, twenty-four perennials (why plant something twice, I reasoned, when for a couple of extra bucks you can do it once and reap the benefits for years?), two tomato plants, and a pot of basil. The more evolved plants, in seeing me coming, folded their leaves, expelled the botanical version of a resigned sigh, and died.

I even toyed with the idea of buying a Japanese maple to replace the tree I killed the summer before. Friends and neighbors would ask, too often and too smugly, "No, really. I'm totally serious. Tell me again how you destroyed a healthy tree?" (If you're serious, why the shit-eating grin?) I had no good answer; it's one of those questions for which no answer makes sense, like why filmmakers remake terrible TV shows from the seventies into even more unbearable feature films. We passed on the tree idea.

When we got home, I convinced my son Colin to do half of the planting, using some unconvincing Hallmark-card bonding message like, "You'll be able to see what we created together every summer until you have kids of your own." I think I even tried to look misty. He wasn't buying it. I believe his words were, "I'm not buying it." Abandoning the warm fuzzies, I told him he had no choice. Ah, the raw power yielded by a parent who doesn't relish getting dirt under his nails.

All of the plants were in the ground when Patty opened the door. "Do those plants require full sun?" What? There are rules? And I was just hearing this now? The warm sweat of my exertion streamed into a new, cold sweat, the whole of which threatened to become a storm front on my face. Was I about to cry? Like when the mother died in *Finding Neverland*, and I tried to hide my emotions, but soon found myself wracked by great, hitching sobs, like a new cast member on *Extreme Makeover: Home Edition*?

Patty repeated the question, then added, "You just planted a bunch of full-sun plants in an area that mostly gets shade. Those chrysanthemums are as good as dead where you've planted them." Wow, bowl me over with your confidence. Now all I could imagine Patty wearing to bed were those impenetrable footie pajamas, with a zipper, not a drop-seat. I asked Patty which ones were the mums. They were, of course, the flowers most shaded. Even an elaborate array of mirrors could only redirect a hint of sunlight into those murky depths.

I tried to argue that, for much of the day, the plants would get *enough* sun; I said this as though I had a clue what I was talking about. I didn't. With gardening, as with marriage, child–rearing and the desire to try new sexual positions, willing something doesn't always translate into making it so.

Fast-forward three weeks. My mums were deader than dead. The flowers, once a vibrant yellow or orange, were now pure black, as were the leaves. They looked like a series of cast-off meatloaves, out of place in their surroundings, like organic Dada art. Cigar butts formed a circle around them, making the whole appear a burnt offering, a grand sacrifice meant to appease the gods of botany. The gods were not appeased, nor was the mother of my kids, who reminded me daily of the eyesore I created.

The hanging plants fared somewhat better. At first, they sagged and pouted, as cherry pink calibrachoas are apparently wont to do (I looked it up), and I felt certain they were accusing me of neglect. However, as the nights became less chilly, and the sun lasted longer each day, they started to thrive. Things were looking up.

Then Patty reminded me, "You'll need to water those every single day to have any hope of keeping them alive." And just like that, things were looking down again. Imminent doom was all around us, and I was to be its harbinger.

I rolled out a modified argument about them getting *enough* water, but, after my failed sun argument, my words felt hollow. Sure enough, if I took a single day off, the plants dripped off the edge of a bone-dry planter. They're supposed to produce hundreds of flowers, but mine played hard to get and offered no more than two dozen the whole summer. Time and again, I'm reminded of Audrey II in *Little Shop of Horrors,* becoming horribly sick whenever its cannibalistic appetite went unfed. I'll stand outside with a hose until my arm falls off, but there's no way I'm pricking my finger and letting these plants suck it dry. When they're watered, they're perky, and have a life that seems, well, almost human. I even do a double-take when I'm convinced they're staring at the back of my head. "Feed me, Brian. Feed me all night long."

The tomatoes also surprised me. Slow to grow at first, my three plants have become a living monstrosity—a hedge, really—clearly visible from blocks away. Our lone pink rose (planted by a previous owner, of course), which once stood with pride between the tiny plants, is now completely obscured; whenever I reach for a tomato, I come away with a gnarled, bloody knuckle. The enormous plants yield fruit at a rate that makes even the rabbits that frequent our yard stop doing what rabbits do long enough to marvel at their rampant reproduction. Everything we serve for dinner now has, of necessity, a distinct tomato theme.

"Dad, really . . . bruschetta again? That's three times this week!"

"Yes, bruschetta again. I will not have lycopene-deficient children." In an argument with kids, it's best to hit them with minor worries cloaked as life-threatening illnesses. "Now pipe down and eat your three-tomato soup before it's too cold to eat. You'll get your pasta when the marinara is ready."

Next to the tomato plants—well, under, really—is the basil. I came to adore this herb, because it grew with minimal attention and just touching it made my hands smell divine. Besides, Mexicans believe it keeps lovers from having a roving eye, so it's a key ingredient of any meal I prepare before we watch a Brad Pitt film. Of course, Patty had to come along and burst my bubble.

"Did you dead-head the basil?"

Excuse me? Did she just reference Jerry Garcia and an herb in the same sentence? From what I know about the sixties, I guess that's not that much of a stretch. But still . . .

"You have to dead-head it." Okay, so my ears hadn't failed me. I wanted to pretend I knew what she was talking about, but the stupefied look on my face betrayed. If I had to guess, I would have said she was making some wry reference to the withered tops of the mums out front.

"If you don't pull the flowers off the plant, the basil will never grow. Too much of the energy needed for the leaves instead goes to the flowers." I knew that.

When I later Googled "Basil Dead Head" just to make sure Patty wasn't messing with me (of course, she wasn't), I learned that ancient Greeks and Romans thought basil would only grow if you cursed like a sailor while sowing the seeds. That may explain my success. And yet, when I hurled similar profanities toward the chrysanthemums, they ignored me.

I took an inventory of my failings—not enough sun for the perennials, not enough water for the hanging plants, and too many flowers for the basil. This could become a full-time commitment, and everyone knows about men and commitment.

All of this attention to the gardens meant the lawn was seldom tended. I would rave about how the flowers were blooming and all Patty could see was the army of thistles and crabgrass that had overtaken the lawn. By the end of the summer, we could ill afford to pull the weeds anymore, because we lacked enough real lawn to hide the giant gaps. Aircraft passing overhead would be convinced we were creating not crop circles but crop Braille.

Exacerbating the lawn problem was our mower's selfish decision to break just as the lawn grew out of control. Okay, to be honest, the mower wasn't totally out of commission, but the self-propulsion mechanism certainly was. I, for one, had no intention of pushing a mower that once pushed itself. I suspect I might find a friendly ally in a certain Milwaukee man who, upon finding his mower wouldn't start, leveled a sawed-off shotgun at the offending appliance and blew it to kingdom come. Turns out the problem wasn't with the mower (at least prior to its summary execution), but with the lack of gas. He may have voided his warranty, but at least he showed it who's boss.

As much as I resented the activities associated with gardening, I enjoyed most of the results. The flowers were gorgeous and full for a week and, with a great infusion of luck, may come back to suffer and die anew before my eyes next year. The tomatoes and basil are delicious, even more so because I played some small part in their creation. We have a new self-propelled lawnmower and, so far, I've had no desire to take potshots at it. In spite of my failures, and my abject stupidity in not following directions (from those with the plants—like the clear instruction, "Plant in full sun"—to those from Patty), I could actually give myself a pat on the back.

Will I do it next year? Of course not. With so many other unrealized ambitions and dreams I'm certain to crush, I try not to make the same mistakes twice. Competence may be a turn-on, but I've taken incompetence to an art.

I Thought I Told You Not to Write About Sex

Patty finishes the last page of a book by Ellen DeGeneres (I don't recall the book's name because lesbians, although smoking hot, write far too little about intercourse), slaps the cover shut, and flips the book on our coffee table with a resounding clunk meant entirely for me. An impressive flourish—usually only approximated on TV spots flogging sports cars—causes the book to spin once on the surface and then stop right before me. Ellen is staring straight into my eyes, and I can't tell yet if she's taking my wife's side in what I know is about to be an "I told you so" moment.

"Done. And *I* was right." You'd be surprised—but she wouldn't—how often she is. "Ellen wrote the whole book without feeling compelled to blather on about sex. I told you so. *I told you.*"

Huh, I didn't see a double "I told you so" coming. If I can't fashion a good retort, and soon, there may be plenty of "Select all, delete" and blind scrambling for story ideas in my immediate future.

"I do hear what you're saying, honey, and I understand." This comes straight out of my active listening classes in college. Unfortunately, Patty attended a better school. Still, I continue.

"But Ellen is crazy famous. She can get away with being funny without being dirty." I try to adopt a wistful, far-away look. "Someday I won't need to get into the behind-closed-doors stuff to sell my books."

I feign distaste at my seeming lack of options; I even think about spitting on the floor (pffft . . . choo!) for emphasis, but Patty would see through my overacting and put the entire debate on hold while I gathered various cleaning products of her choosing—disinfectant cleanser, paper towels, a mop, and such—and remove all evidence of the offending sputum. It could be *hours* before we got back on track.

"But I'm not a household name, Patty, you know that." She knows. If I was, we'd be living in a much more expansive house without peeling paint, dead plants, and broken downspouts, and with a full staff of help to dispatch insects or overbearing friends upon arrival. "So my best chance—no, I would say my *only* chance—to write your kind of dull, sex-free book someday is to bite the bullet now."

Have my woebegone expression and tone convinced her, now, how it pains me to talk at length about my absolute favorite thing in the entire world? Does she accept that my reluctant hand has been forced by circumstances none can control—or is she still savvy to my utter inability to keep my mind, and my keyboard, out of the gutter? I don't know. I press forward, like the second in line at a book signing for *The Complete Idiot's Guide to Lemmings*.

I try, "So you found *one* book in all the books in the entire universe that doesn't talk about sex. What about David Sedaris? And Augusten Burroughs? They've never shied away from talking about this stuff—they'll even mention fellatio." I let this last word roll off my tongue like drool—*fuhhh . . . leeeeaaaay . . . shee . . . ohhh*—thinking I sound both suave and cerebral. Besides, by using the scientific term, instead of just blurting out "blow job," I've fooled myself into thinking that seeming serious and analytical will better cement my case.

Patty walks away, murmuring something under her breath that sounds like, "I'm going to fetch a knife and chop off your penis," but I pretend I don't hear her. If I challenge her, and all she was really saying was, "Women really do come from Venus," I'll look like I'm as paranoid as I was the last time she was out to get me. Still, I concede the argument.

Having lost the battle but unprepared to concede the war, I can still pull a trick or two out of my sleeve. Rather than delve further into the happenings and non-happenings in the bedroom I share today, I can instead whirl you back in time, long before Patty, and give you a peek under the sheets of my childhood. You may want to pack an umbrella. And perhaps a moist towelette.

Still there? As I'm writing this, I'm recalling the kids' story, *The Monster at the End of the Book*, where Grover of Sesame Street fame begs the reader not to flip each page because it brings them closer to the terrifying monster—which turns out, to everyone's shock, to be lovable, furry old Grover himself. (Sorry for not providing a spoiler alert.) I'm worrying anyone who's already had a glimpse into my psyche will say, "Enough, enough, enough. I get it. The monster at the end of his book is going to be him, tipped back in a rocking chair, buck naked with his hairy legs behind his ears." Don't fret. As I'm writing this, I'm never forgetting my own mother might be reading it.

Okay, let's talk masturbation. Still there? Good. Girls, pour yourself a glass of white wine and hunker down—you're going to journey into the dark, damp psyche of your boyfriend, husband, or son. Could you grab a glass for my mom? Gents, welcome back to your repressed memories; I'll be your server today.

Every boy discovers, from the first time he inventories his body parts, that if he fiddles enough with his little doo-hickey, it becomes as rigid as an overcooked Vienna sausage—useless for the time being, really, but rigid nonetheless. Some women would no doubt argue it *remains* useless, but that's another debate. Countless hours can be wasted in the bathtub pushing said stiffy under the water as far as possible, releasing it, and then squealing with delight as it snaps back to, and through, the surface, causing a glorious plume of soapy water to launch high into the air. I take showers now, and not baths, or I would still do this today.

The next phase of the journey toward personal discovery (a tame synonym for "becoming a chronic masturbator") is involuntary and more than a trifle unsettling. This is the infamous for-absolutely-no-reason hard-on. For most, it happens in church, in the dentist's chair, on local transit, at school, whenever slow dancing ("Stairway to Heaven" was a guaranteed eleven-minute boner), when snooping with your friend at your friend's sister, and any moment a boy is either awake or unconscious. For me it first happened, in true stereotypical fashion, in my freshman biology class. Deep in thought as I compiled notes from that day's dissection project, I suddenly came to the unmistakable realization that I wasn't alone. I hadn't thought about a girl. The teacher wasn't standing before a chart of female genitalia, using a pointer to trace the path through the vaginal canal or discussing the finer nuances of the clitoral hood. I had just disemboweled a worm, for God's sake—how sexy is that? (If you have any answer to this question, please keep it to yourself.)

What transforms bad into worse here is that as soon as I was aware of the situation, it locked in. Like reruns of bad sitcoms, my alter ego just wouldn't go away. You've seen the commercials that advise you to seek medical attention if you experience an erection lasting more than four hours? In spite of the jokes, those aren't happy men. Based on this recommendation, I should have been a regular fixture (oh, you know what I mean) at the doctor's office, or a sundial in my parents' backyard.

At roughly the same age you're hosting thrice-daily surprise parties in your pants—twelve, thirteen, maybe fourteen if you're so brain dead you don't realize a benevolent spirit has just smiled upon you—your mind becomes a moving collage of confusing thoughts, all choreographed to the lusty beats of Carmina Burana. The nightmare you once had about being caught naked in a school cloakroom is now a wild fantasy about stripping in the cloakroom with any girl from the class, all of whom have, overnight, become inexplicably and scaldingly hot. These same girls who, just weeks before, you wanted to throw something *at,* you now want to throw something *in*. Even replacing a bulb in a lamp makes you crave a post-bulbing cigarette. So, to silence these incessant voices, instinct forces you to take matters into your own hands.

For reasons I'll never grasp (there I go again), my first true sexual self-realization took place one afternoon in the basement of my childhood home, while I was taking in the latest installment of *The Undersea World of Jacques Cousteau*. I'd like to believe some Freudian trigger was at play here—perhaps I was affected by images of a giant steel ship parting waves—but I know there was nothing of the sort. I was watching the show, and absentmindedly fiddling when I had what some call "an awakening." This awakening would, of necessity, be a part of my daily existence for the next—let's see—twenty-nine years . . . and counting.

What starts out as a somewhat guilty, pubescent pleasure soon becomes an obsession indulged with no shame and little modesty. And then things deteriorate. Everyone you've ever encountered becomes a target for your secret lust. Your teachers. Everyone you see on television. The lady who cuts your hair, who happens to be the mother of one of your best friends. The mothers and sisters of all your best friends. Their aunts, cousins, friends of cousins, third cousins twice removed on the paternal side. Your own cousins. The old lady down the street whose lawn you mow and who you presumed had not invaded anyone's fantasies in a good long time. Every person you see in church (which is now easier to get through, because instead of thinking about God you're conducting a ranked inventory of who you'd like to violate—a dirty to-do list.) The lady who someone once told you was a swinger; you didn't know what that even meant, but it sounded cool so she made the list. The neighbor a few houses down who you heard had made a comment about, "Oh, if it wasn't illegal, what I'd do to him"—a comment that may not have even been true, but which now is the greatest compliment you've ever received. You soon realize that as long as you're doing this in your head (and, to be accurate, in your hand), nothing is so vulgar you can't indulge it.

Herein lies the rub: as teenage boys, we're so delighted at this gift that has fallen from the heavens into our laps, we don't keep it to ourselves. We celebrate it. We talk about it with our friends. If you're hosting a sleepover and the urge hits to burp the worm (one of the many terms for male masturbation, my new favorite being, "Calling down for more mayo"), there's an unwritten law, an instinct even, that says, "We all know what I'm doing over on this side of the room because you're doing the same over there. Don't say anything, because it will kill the mood, and as a thirteen-year-old, I don't want to invest the four seconds it will take to start this up again."

But, later, over smuggled cigarettes, six packs of butterscotch pudding, and big bottles of New Coke (you had to be there), you talk. And you share with your friends all the people you've violated in the sex club that is your brain, using caution to omit the names of their siblings. One friend told me once he had thought about my mom. My first response was, "Oh my God, why?" This not because I was offended he pictured himself doing unspeakable things to the person who gave me life and tended all my nosebleeds, but because I just couldn't fathom anyone being attracted to my mom—even my dad. I'm not saying my mom was unattractive—in fact, there are times when, to a boy, his mother is the most beautiful person in the world—but nobody should ever want to do *that* to *your* mom. And then, once the reality of what he said sunk in, I did start taking offense. So, to break the tension, and to steer my friend's thinking off my mom, I responded, "Yeah, well, I put my hand in your sister's undies."

The other danger in being too candid about what's going on in your head is that you have little control over what's happening in there. I think we're all just a hair's breadth away from either becoming the next da Vinci or the next Dahmer. Some nasty shit goes down in the young male brain. Fortunately, we outgrow this.

One day, my friend Derek and I were sitting in his backyard, trying to decide whether to hunt frogs or drink some of his parents' concord grape wine, when Derek came up with another idea. "You know, we could go upstairs and jerk off next to each other and have a race to see who could finish first." Now, I know some of you are thinking, "Where were the parents?" and others might say, "If you break the tape in a race toward premature ejaculation, does anyone really win?" But, at the time, his question seemed reasonable, if not just a smidge awkward. I didn't want to, which told me that, in spite of thinking I sounded effeminate when recorded on tape, I could be that much more confident I wasn't going to wake up one morning and discover I was gay, which was of supreme import even to gay teenagers in those days.

So, while I wasn't flattered, I also wasn't offended. He did push things too far, though, when before getting my go-ahead on the contest, he added, "And when we're finished"—which told me that even if there was a winner, we were both expected to run the whole race—"We can have the dog clean it up." I looked at him. He looked at me. I waited for him to laugh. He didn't laugh. As soon as he realized I wasn't about to drop my Levis, grab my crotch, and yell, "Last one there is a dirty rotten egg," he shook his head and went on the attack. "Oh my god, I can't believe you even thought about that, you fucking faggot." I'm decades older, but still I'm flummoxed by this logic.

But that's just it. Teenage boys have no logic. Almost all experience something that would now be given a label like obsessive-compulsive disorder, or attention-deficit disorder, or some other term designed to package the maelstrom of hormones that guide our every waking (and sleeping) moment. To an extent, it's true. Everything becomes about sex. Everything.

For the first time in your life, instead of saying to the neighborhood girl, "We should build a fort so we can have a farting contest," you start saying, "We should build a fort so we can . . ." And I'll let you fill in your own ending. For myself, I was going to say, "talk about feelings," but I suspect most of you simply thought, "fuck." It's insidious. Your seventh-grade teacher screams inches from your face and you cannot pass up the opportunity to look down her blouse. You start wondering what positions people use, including—and if there is a hell, I'm sure this just got me a mayoral seat there—your parents. You don't want to think about this stuff, but you can't shut up the voices, oh the many voices, trumpeting and blaring and screaming and wailing in your head.

And soon we're not content to just grab ourselves and go to town. We find ourselves becoming creative. We use our non-throwing hand. We try to use both hands but, unless you're more blessed than I, we must alternate rather than combine. We use our hands facing the other direction, like a dollar-store reverse cowgirl. We try to reach it with our mouths (most of us don't even get close, but if you've ever met a guy who said he wouldn't if he could, you've just met a liar).

My brother, a natural do-it-yourselfer in every sense of the word, once fashioned a masturbation device out of a Maxwell House jar, half a dozen sandwich bags, a quarter roll of cellophane tape and a half cup of Vaseline. He offered to loan it to me; there was just no way. I don't care how "gently used" it was, I wanted none of that. I did, however, accept his loan of *100 Pages of Raven-Haired Pussy,* a magazine I appreciated not only for its dimensions but also for its truth in advertising.

My younger brother Paul, whose Asperger's syndrome didn't exempt him from normal adolescent urges, was also creative. He shared with me that his preferred method was to make love to the gap between the mattress and box spring of his bed. Ready to take notes about what seemed like an intriguing new possibility, I asked him what he used for lubricant. He just stared at me. I said, "Paul, if you didn't use Vaseline or vegetable oil or something, you must have sheared off half the skin on your penis!" At which he gave a long, throaty, and naughty chuckle and said, simply, "Y . . . yeah." That was our last-ever conversation about masturbation.

When, at fifteen, I moved from a small village of 1,500 to a booming metropolis of 15,000, we also moved from antenna to cable, which was almost as exciting as the discovery of what I came to think of as New-penis. First, there were channels that didn't bleep out "fuck" or "shit," which seemed like an honor for some reason, and some even showed boobies and pubes.

Second, if you stayed up late enough on a Friday or Saturday night, the multicultural channel showed Italian movies, almost all of which followed the same formula: Man meets woman. Man has sex with woman. Woman yells at man. Man in turn yells at woman. Man and woman make up. Man and woman have make-up sex. Rinse and repeat. It didn't make one speck of difference that the only words I understood in ninety minutes were "ciao" and "rrrrha-ha." If I had never discovered girls, I'd still be watching today, and would be more fluent in Italian than anyone who's gone the Rosetta Stone route.

This masturbatory trend continued and, surprise, surprise, I'm not blind, my growth was not stunted, and I don't have hair on my palms. If wanking really put hair on your palms, mine would look like Robin Williams' chest. True, I may be insane, but I blame that on drug experimentation, not diddling.

Many men would like you to believe masturbation is an embarrassing secret they've left in the past, and that, as the proverb says, when they became a man they put away childish things. The stats don't bear this out. The best numbers I could find suggest that 90 percent of men and 65 percent of women master their own domains with some regularity. Perhaps sex educator Sue Johanson summed it up best when she quipped, "Ninety-nine percent of men of all ages masturbate regularly, and the other 1 percent are liars." She doesn't mean the fraction of a percent who masturbate to a dangerous degree of obsession; she doesn't mention me at all.

Still, I think my libido may seem tame next to that of my older brother, masturbation-machine inventor and as truthful an observer of his own needs as one will ever find. When he was a teenager, he maintained under his bed the world's largest—and perhaps most unabashedly vulgar—collection of clipped images of naked women, organized and categorized in seven large photo albums. Yes, categorized, so he could have at hand (heh heh) whatever particular variety of kink inspired him at a given moment. I'm not a betting man, but I would say chances are good you'd find these same albums, and others too vulgar to sit next to the under-the-bed seven, on his night table (or, in a nod to propriety, in his closet) today—along with hundreds upon hundreds of discarded white athletic socks.

I was a wadded-tissue man myself. Or I *became* one, after my mother called me to the laundry room and chided, "Would you please knock it off? I just tried to load your sheets in the washer and they snapped." Messages such as this from one's mother provide a strong impetus for change. Of course, she was no happier when she looked behind my bed and found a snow-white mountain of paper, and an answer as to why she was buying four jumbo packs of Cottonelle every week. I think she *did* like it when I left home. I haven't been invited to move back.

Through my teenage years, taking care of business became as essential a part of every day as food, candy bars, and bottled soda, and my appetite for each was legendary. I presume girls were doing some of the same things—I've heard rumors about the bathtub faucet, the pulsating shower massager, and the back of an electric toothbrush—but I doubt with the same level of unabashed commitment. Women, though, will admit to what they've done and do, even if they won't talk about it in the graphic detail we men would prefer. However, many adult men, for some reason, have taken something perfectly natural (and, I would add, naturally perfect) and turned it into a negative equation: for some, masturbation equals weakness. For the less evolved, masturbation equals fag.

My former neighbor Mark sadly existed in both camps. Let me explain.

Mark and I became second-time fathers at the same time, and had each agreed we had done our share of expanding the human race. Mark's wife felt that two tours of duty through the war zone were all she would enlist for. This stance became quite evident when, one evening, Mark jumped up from my picnic table and said, "I'm going to go have sex. Michelle's on her period." I didn't at first grasp the one-to-one correlation, especially since it sounded like a preference, so I asked what he meant. He said, "She'll only do it when she's on her period, because she's afraid she'll get pregnant." I had heard far more than enough, so I walked him to the door.

As for me, as much as I loved just about everything about being a father that didn't involve body waste, screaming, or ultimate responsibility for the child's safety, I just knew that if a third kid came along, no amount of histrionics would get me off the hook for frequent diaper changes—no gagging, retching, simpering, or wrapping sweatshirts around my nose and mouth. So Mark and I both decided to have vasectomies. Not side by side—that would be way too creepy and familiar—but within a couple of months of each other. I went first.

After Mark had his procedure, and had completed the requisite bag-of-peas-on-crotch recovery phase during which men take no visitors, we met over a beer to compare notes. He was comfortable with his choice, but seemed troubled about the immediate future.

Mark:I have to go back for a check-up, to make sure everything worked. I'm freaking out.

Me:Why? It's no big deal. They give you a couple of racy magazines and a paper cup, you do your thing, and then you wait for the results.

Mark: ....That's just it. I've never done *that* before.

Me:....................Never done what? Huh . . . ? Oh. You haven't? [Here you have to say the words while in the background harmonizing a constant *Hahahahahahahahahaha*.] You say you've *never* . . . Oh, just a minute, can't breathe. No, no, no, please stop . . . are you serious?

Mark:I'm totally serious. I don't do that, and I never have. It's gay. [Okay, then I'm the gayest person ever.]

I never understood this about my generation. Anything someone didn't like was always "gay." Wrestling with your friends at age eight? Best friends always. Wrestling with your friends at age fourteen? Gay. Taking a sip out of the same can of cream soda when you were age eight? Best friends always, and fiscally responsible. At fifteen, taking a sip of the same can of anything with the word "cream"? Gayer than gay. And yet the same people who had no problem deciding your sexual orientation on a whim thought nothing about the rich subtext in insults like, "Why don't you blow me, you fag?"

So, as a friend and lover of learning, I offered to tell Mark about the wonderful world of wanking. He wasn't interested, but we'll still keep him in the club, because to us he'll always be a wanker.

I've met many Marks since then. Each was a classic example of a person to whom psychologists refer to as "in denial." He also falls into the category of what I call delusional, bold-faced pathological liars. Like some of my friends who, while mopping up their third spilled cocktail of the evening, say they've never had drinking issues. Or other guys who boast about their prowess or endowment while, behind their heads, their wives roll their eyes. Instead of crafting façades to dress up something they're not, I think these people need to learn to love themselves.

As often and as shamelessly as necessary.

Victory and De-Feet

This past weekend, while Patty and I ran errands with our two youngest kids, we stopped for lunch at Portillo's, a fast-food chain renowned in the Midwest for its Italian beef sandwiches and hot dogs, and for the sheer genius that married a chocolate milkshake *and* chocolate cake into a single beverage. Bear in mind that 85 percent of Chicago restaurants claim the tastiest beef, most palate-pleasing hot dogs, and better-than-you-could-ever-imagine pizza, so the term "renowned" is tossed about liberally. (I'll let you in on a little secret: the best pizza in the universe hails not from Chicago, New York, or any other metropolis, but from my childhood home of 2,000 pizza-spoiled citizens—Colborne, Ontario, Canada. Tell the folks at Vito's Brian sent you.)

Patty seldom passes on an opportunity to dine out—not because fast food is her favorite dining experience, but because seeing French fries drop to someone else's floor is preferable to finding cold, mashed residue on our own. We had settled in at our booth, and I was readying to bury my face into my bacon cheeseburger—a favorite pastime, long mastered—when my daughter Kelly stopped time.

"Mom, oh my God . . ." Here on display was the teenage girl's requisite flair for the dramatic, used with equal emphasis for real emergencies, like being broadsided by a city bus or running low on eye shadow, and for any and all minor situations, like I hoped this would be. "Dad was just *totally* checking that woman out."

My burger fell with a dull plop on the wrapper in front of me. Alarm bells clanged throughout my head. *Red alert, red alert.* My face, now drained of blood, adopted my best "Who? Me?" look. My daughter ignored my feeble attempt at self-preservation. She nodded accusingly, "Yes, you," and then pointed, with a stiff arm and even stiffer finger, to the poor, helpless woman it seems I'd so shamelessly violated. For a second I thought about popping the cyanide capsule I keep in my pocket for such occasions.

"No, don't worry, Mom. He wasn't gawking at her ass or anything." Like this distinction might get me off this giant, body-rending hook. "He was looking at her *feet.*"

I didn't want to look at Patty. I wanted to look anywhere but at Patty. I wanted to gaze up at the ceiling and change the subject to anything other than my impending death.

"Look, kids, an antique bicycle! And license plates. Have you ever seen a Texas plate from the thirties before? It's really quite breathtaking."

But, in the dreadful silence that boomed in after Kelly's salvo, my infernal eyes betrayed me. I didn't want to look at Patty, but Patty *did* want to look at me. My eyes inched toward hers, and then were sucked in by her tractor beam, a Death Star for husbands. With an expression that conveyed both bemusement and a hint of agitation, Patty said, "Again, Brian? *Again?*"

Guilty as charged.

Let's just say it: I'm a podophile. Before you pound down my door at nightfall with an angry posse wielding torches and pitchforks—"Burn the reprobate rapist!"—check the spelling. I'm not attracted in any way, shape or form to children. At this moment,

I'm not even fond of one of the kids I've loved and nurtured, who has just merrily taken the wheel of the bus that ploughed right into me.

So, I don't dig kids. Instead, I am madly, gloriously—and, it would seem, obviously—obsessed with feet.

As much as I love the autumn, with its glorious colors and refreshing cool evenings, I mourn the passing of summer. Sure, I miss the picnic table meals, ice cream breaks, trips to the local waterpark, and my favorite outdoor peeing spot, right next to the air conditioner. I miss the neighbors who in the warmer months drop in on a whim, drink until they vomit in our laundry basket, and then destroy whatever happens to be the most expensive thing in our home they haven't yet broken. I even feel a twinge of melancholy when the long days start to recede and the nights start again just after dinner. There's something terribly depressing about seeing your kids come home from school by moonlight.

But what I miss more than anything—more than baseball, even, as the season winds down—is summer footwear (or lack thereof). I miss my world of bare tootsies on beaches; on a good day, it's like a chocoholic's shopping spree at a Fannie May shop. In every supermarket, someone has to reach up to a high shelf, thus exposing a long expanse of sole atop five delicately scrunched digits. I just stand there, offering no assistance whatsoever. And—still my beating heart—how about feet sticking provocatively out car windows? Art, pure art.

As the summer fades, Patty and I will plan a night out, and I'll be ready to help pick one of my favorite pairs of sandals from the dozens I've forced upon her. I'll then be devastated when she opts for socks and boots because her feet might get cold. Can't someone come up with a sandal that warms the feet while keeping them exposed? I'll buy a closetful, I promise.

"There can't be more than six inches of snow on the ground. Don't you think knee-length boots are a bit extreme?" My argument fails. "What if I carry you to and from the car? What if I get down on my knees and beg? What if I threaten you?" And still, nothing works.

According to the *MisterPoll,* an online survey site, only 5 percent of men list feet as their favorite female body part. Most of my friends are more garden-variety—these are your boob men (26%) and ass men (21%). Don't get me wrong, I'm fond of tits and tushies, but they just don't inspire glorious fantasies like a well-tended set of soles. Besides, it's harder to ogle these areas without getting punched. Among this particular sample, one-fifth went so far as to rate feet as their least-favorite body part. That's just crazy. Ears look goofy on just about everyone; why not center them out for ridicule?

Still, I know I'm not alone. In 2006, America Online (AOL) published a database of search terms most often submitted by subscribers. Of all searches that included the word "fetish," the greatest number also included the word "foot." Even if you exclude the several thousand times I've been the one conducting the search, there must be others out there.

Consider also the endless number of Web sites devoted to this phenomenon. On top of your standard, catch-all sites that appeal to fans of feet in general are subsets for the kinkier among us. Just scanning through Google results I imagine the work days that could be pissed away seeking out soles and toes that are exotic, lovely, cute, hot, Scandinavian, tasty, exquisite, sweet, sexy, filthy, perfect, dreamy, manic, and angel-kissed. I even found more extreme sites that promised feet that were footalicious, cummy (yuck . . . but I'd still look), and even fruity. Fruity? The best was the site that boasted it contained only *real* sexy feet. This is, I presume, to distinguish those who prefer the organic version to prosthetics.

"Hey, babe. If you're heading up to bed early, would you mind hopping? You'll do me a solid if you could just leave your leg on the coffee table. I'll give it back this time, and without teeth marks or other biohazard, I promise."

To be honest, I don't know how I became a fan of feet. Researchers have observed that foot fetishism, as a phenomenon, increases in prevalence during historical periods in which sexually transmitted diseases are at their strongest. I can say, with some certainty, that I don't fear syphilis on a daily basis, but that doesn't keep me from staring with my mouth open when someone throws their bare feet up on a picnic table. If looking at feet caused disease, I'd be too dead right now to expound upon my foot thing. But it doesn't, so that won't explain it. A neurologist, Vilayanur Ramachandran, suggested that feet and genitals occupy adjacent sections of the somatosensory cortex. This means my brain may just be coming up with the equation: foot equals vagina. This seems more reasonable, because while I'm pro-foot, to be sure, I'm not at all *anti*-vagina.

My first recall of noticing feet came when my parents hired a babysitter when I was no more than five years old. Her name was Bilanca, and a more useless babysitter one would be hard-pressed to find. Bilanca would lay out in our yard in her bikini, catching rays and doing nothing babysitters typically do—feeding us, for starters—and I would sit for hours at the end of the lounger staring at her soles and toes. I did this with such relish and so little modesty that there was once a photo in the family album of Bilanca, her feet, and me—staring at her feet. To this day, I wonder who snapped it—perhaps a kindred spirit?

I'm sure I wanted to tuck my fingertips under the delicate tops of Bilanca's toes, but I couldn't build up the nerve. Perhaps, had I thrown caution to the wind, she might have kicked me squarely in the nose and the fetish would have been knocked out of me. Nope.

Sadly, my devotion to the southernmost region of Bilanca's geography was not enough in my parent's thinking to make up for her questionable child-care skills, so our sitter, glorious piggies and all, was history. My love for feet, and my memories of hers, was not.

When most people hear about my lifelong obsession, they come back with, "Oh, you wouldn't like *my* feet. They're disgusting." More often than not, though, they're wrong. Send me a picture if you want to be sure; I doubt I'll send a reply letter, but out of courtesy I'll hold on to your thoughtful gift. Still, it's true— some feet out there are a bit hard even on my adoring eyes. Short feet with chubby toes hold no magic, nor do soles that look like the bottoms of work boots (like mine do). Other turn-offs in the foot arena include those that have botflies popping in and out of them like whack-a-moles, any whose aroma hints of death (completed or imminent), or the feet of *my* parents and grandparents. But most women, from age eighteen to eighty-one, and all the years between, have botfly-free feet that deserve at least a passing glance.

So you may be asking yourself, "I know now what makes for a shitty foot; what makes for a good one?" Well, I'm glad you asked. The best have longer-than-average, somewhat-square toes, long, high arches, square toenails that are freshly polished, and a nice, shiny ball. If they wrinkle on the soles, like a newborn baby's bottom or former President Carter's face, even better. Patty's are perfect. So perfect, in fact, that she's spawned a subset of my naughty vice. Try as I might to contain the urge, I can't keep myself from biting the foot that feeds me.

"Ow. Ow. Owww! Stop that! It's not nice for me at all. It just hurts." The toes disappear under a blanket, like ruby slippers retreating under Dorothy's house.

"You *give* those back." They may be attached to her but, as far as I'm concerned, they're my property, and she has stolen them.

"No way. I won't do it. You'll just bite them again."

"But I won't."

"But you *will.* You say you won't, but you always do."

"I won't this time. I promise."

Two minutes later: "Ow. Ow. Ow!" This time, they're gone for good.

Bilanca, wherever you are, I have a babysitting job for you. The kids will be fed and occupied with other things; besides, they're all too old for a babysitter. I don't care. You can just lie out in the sun and do nothing at all. I don't even care that you must be pushing sixty. As before, you need not worry about feeding anyone. You didn't realize it at the time, when I slobbered all over you like an overheated St. Bernard, but you somehow touched this lad's soul. If only I had found the nerve to tickle yours.

Immaculate Misconceptions

While squirming through *Crucifixion,* a History Channel offering Patty and I watched one evening, it occurred to me that the process of death-by-cross, while effective, could not have been fun.

Long before the unfortunate victim even sees the cross, soldiers scourge him with bone-adorned whips called flagrums that rend the skin and shred vital organs, leaving the recipient with mortal injuries. The only comparable pain I've experienced came from eating over-spiced chili on an unsettled morning-after stomach; without putting too fine a point on it, that shit tore me up.

After a vigorous flogging, the condemned lugs a heavy crosspiece on his shoulders for some distance while being bombarded with harsh words and harsher stones. I whine if forced to carry bags of groceries from the car to our house—because that's what kids are for—so I'd take issue with neighbors adding injury to insult by pelting me with rocks.

"Hey! Stop that!" A duck, a bob, a weave. "Stop . . . ow . . . it really hurts!"

Call me oversensitive. I've been called worse. Often.

After the scourging and stoning, as if *this* wasn't enough, soldiers nail the victim through the feet and wrists (not through the hands, as this would tear through, causing the victim to fall forward into an undignified, ass-up pose that wouldn't look at all impressive in Renaissance art). Here he dangles until his lungs fill with snot and saliva. Over hours or days, he slowly drowns. When I see this level of torture, I find myself wondering why women boast childbirth is the most painful thing a person can experience. Really, from where I sit, it doesn't seem like it could be *that* bad. Like a nasty hangnail, or finding a fingernail (or a finger) in your food after you've finished two-thirds of it. If you think about it, isn't childbirth really like reverse sexual intercourse with a startlingly well-endowed partner?

Still, and at the risk of sounding inappropriate, I think I have a fair appreciation of profound suffering. No, I haven't been scourged. I've never been stoned (not with rocks, anyway). None of even my wildest weekends—you know, the ones so out of control you only find out about them anecdotally from friends of now-former friends—included being nailed to a cross. But just this past weekend, I did endure profound suffering, complete with a great wailing and gnashing of teeth. Of course, I'm recalling one of those life-altering ordeals every man, against every fiber of his being, must one day face. No, not shopping for shoes, although this falls a close second, followed by being caught masturbating next to a wife you were sure was asleep ("Stop that!").

No, this past weekend, I made what I considered a supreme sacrifice.

I attended my wife's co-worker's wedding.

I understand weddings have their high points. First and foremost is free booze. This would have been great, and alone worth the trip, but both Patty and I had opted against drinking at the reception because we're both trying to shed a few pounds. So, instead, we were left to mope in a sober depression (like Christ on the cross, I thought) while all our tablemates made alcohol-fueled jokes that may have seemed droll if we were smashed, but, since we weren't liquored up, weren't funny at all.

One guest expounded at length about what she perceived to be the wonders of pigs' milk, since Dolly Parton, while lost as a child, had apparently been found suckling on a sow's teat. Our storyteller even made the big-boobs gesture because, as a man, I wouldn't have been able to picture giant breasts without a supporting visual. I couldn't wait to hear more, but instead I just went out for a smoke until the subject changed. On my way out, one guest from overseas asked if I could direct him to the "cludgey." I presumed he meant bathroom, but since he spoke not in real words but colloquialisms, I just shook my head in a superior fashion and left.

The second perk of weddings is an iron-clad guarantee of getting lucky. I don't know what dormant hormone gushes through the female brain at a wedding, but I'm not one to sucker-punch a gift horse in the mouth. Somehow, even we old married guys get crazy-monkey sex—and without begging—after attending a wedding. I knew I was locked in the second time I heard Patty say "Aw . . ." with a dreamy gel-lensed swoon, in response to some tidbit of tender schlock. Patty's not typically sentimental, but there she was, suckling on the sow's teat of romance. After a good wedding, even chronic masturbators rest their wrists for a night.

Beyond that, weddings mostly suck.

What especially sucks is what I call Small Purse Syndrome. In the real world, women carry handbags large enough to stash anything and everything they might ever need for any situation, such as life in a post-apocalyptic world. In a fair and just society, they also leave enough spare space for a husband's keys, cigarettes, lighter, wallet, cell phone, crack pipe and such. But when fashion dictates the carrying of a small purse, these conventions are turned on their ear. The Small Purse Syndrome solves this problem by transferring all of the contents of the purse to the pockets of the man's suit, which makes her look elegant and delicate. He looks like he's crapped such a mother lode it's squirted up both sides of his jacket.

The wedding and reception were both held in a hotel. If you must suffer through a day of others' greatest happiness, convenience eases the sting. We arrived close (too close) to the time of the wedding and, since I deemed it important to check on the score of the baseball game once more before the happy couple exchanged vows, I only made it back in time by sprinting back into the room, cutting off the bridesmaids in the process.

When seated, I noticed that a single female co-worker of Patty's had brought, as her "date," another female co-worker of Patty's. I nudged Patty. She tried to ignore me, so I punched her in the arm.

"Ow. What?"

"Check it out."

"Check out what?"

"Laura brought Jen."

"I see that."

"God, I hope they make out."

A male friend of mine, sitting next to me, nodded. Patty's eyes rolled back out of her head just as the bride entered the room. She looked tall, slim and, of course, lovely, as most women do when they've sunk thousands of dollars into presenting themselves as the ultimate trophy for the very last time. After that it's all sweatpants, listen to me drone on about my day, catty remark, catty remark, I want you to change, bitch, bitch, bitch.

The groom was, to put it delicately, diminutive. Here he was, signing away his share of the house in a near-inevitable future divorce settlement, and yet he wouldn't pass the height requirement for anything but the kiddie rides at Six Flags. At least he would be forever spared having to get up off the sofa to reach for a bowl from the top shelf of a kitchen cabinet. And, of course, whenever he wanted to show affection, much to the joy of his wife, he'd be able to innocently bury his face into her cleavage. These are perks, although it would stink to wear a dress shirt with a bulldozer and the word "Tonka" on the back.

Still, one doesn't often see the bride towering over the groom, and I found myself wondering what drew her toward her wee Toulouse. That changed the first time he opened his mouth. I feel a trifle uncomfortable saying this, but his deep, rich British accent melted me. He could have told the whole gathering to fuck themselves and they would have nodded, with a dreamy look, and muttered, "Sure thing." I turned to my male friend again.

"Oh my god, don't take this the wrong way, but for just a second there, I'm pretty sure I was gay."

To which he replied, with hesitation or offense, "I know, right? Did it just get hotter in here?"

I spent most of the ceremony stroking Patty's kneecap to convince myself I hadn't switched teams. It was a close call, to be sure, but I'm still the starting quarterback on Team Vagina.

After the wedding, which included all your standard vows most married couples break faster than New Year's resolutions, we were ushered into the lobby, where drinks I couldn't drink and appetizers I couldn't appetize upon paraded past us, which again made me think about what Jesus must have endured. So, instead of even trying to enjoy myself, I killed a half hour critically appraising everyone else in the room. *Fat, fat, pretty, old, bad toupée, fat, woof, bet he can't get it up, coffin makeup, not bad, fat, she doesn't look happy with him (oh, that's Patty), fat.*

I had just commented to Patty about liking one woman's dress and another's shoes when I turned to catch my aforementioned male friend, head askew, looking at me with an awkward grimace.

"How sure are you about that gay thing?"

(I don't exactly know how, but Patty somehow brainwashed me into noticing fashion. I appreciate nice clothes both on [and off] women. I think most men secretly do. I even know what taffeta and tuck-pointing are. Most guys, however, also know enough not to share their impressions aloud. I once made a similar comment in our local dive hangout about the attractive design of a woman's purse. The bearded biker guy in the wife-beater t-shirt next to me fixed me with a gaze that conveyed at once sadness, disgust, and fear. He pleaded, "Please don't.")

Almost everyone we spoke to was a teacher, like Patty. One, who works in Patty's department, complained at length to Patty about how her open-toed shoes were uncomfortable across her soles and ankles, how painting her nails was a chore, and about how her toes were mashed together inside. She giggled and punched me on the shoulder, offering, "Well that's a major T.M.I., I guess," before walking away. Patty, who understands my dirty little secret about feet (and wasn't thrilled about how elated I looked), also pleaded, "Please don't."

We stayed later than many of the guests, I think in part to relish the novelty of seeing people bombed into oblivion without even the remotest buzz ourselves. Normally, Patty would be ushering me to the door much earlier, saying, "He was joking about taking the wedding night photos. And no, he wasn't really offering to hold your ankles. He gets like this sometimes." For tonight at least, I could be holier-than-thou.

Just before we left, one guest, who had taken full advantage of the open bar, told us, in a less-melting English accent/slur, that we couldn't leave. She looked broad enough to tackle me. I explained that since we didn't have a room, we'd need to get home. Without hesitation, she offered the other double bed in her room if we would just stick around. I wasn't sure if the wedding-sex phenomenon that turned good girls into shameless sluts also transformed married folk into no-holds-barred swingers, but I wasn't sticking around to find out. In yet another light bulb moment, I came up with an excuse.

"I snore."

Patty nodded vigorously. "He really does."

To which our bleary-eyed attacker shrieked, "That's lovely, pet. I snore toooooo . . ." She followed this with a cackle and an enormous drunken hug from arms I thought were too ample for her sleeveless chiffon evening gown. Burned earlier for speaking aloud, I kept this fashion observation to myself.

Weighted down with a full complement of everything Patty has ever taken anywhere, and fearing that hesitation would mean I would also need to bear the weight of a drunken Brit as well—like the aforementioned cross—I beat a hasty retreat through the door, to my car, and home where, from the depths of suffering, and with a howl borne of my ancestry, I might rise again.

Going Green

I'll just bet when you read this chapter's title you thought, "Oh, great. A tree hugger. Here comes a boast about basting in his own funk for weeks, eating nothing but bark beetles and eagle droppings, all the while refusing to leave his perch atop a giant redwood." Nope. You won't hear me preach about my lifelong sense of social responsibility, nor will you roll your eyes as I laud myself as a thoughtful and cautious steward of the environment.

No, I pretty much just *kill* things—like household plants, any flavor in meals, and most of my kids' dreams of a well-adjusted future. And I own (of necessity, with a family of seven) an enormous, gas-and-clean-air guzzling SUV. What's more, I only recycle because I can't find room in our garbage cart for the hundreds of Diet Coke cans I dispatch each week—so they go, out of convenience more than conscience, into the giant recycling bin our town council provided for us. So I'm no environmental activist, although I will admit *An Inconvenient Truth* rattled me enough to give me pause before tossing copious amounts of plastic into my outdoor fire pit. Al Gore, you need not acknowledge me in public; we're all just trying to play our part.

As much as I'd like to heap laurels upon myself for my world-saving mentality, I'm referring not to green spaces, but to my green card. You see, I didn't always hail from the home of the brave—I'm originally a small-town boy from the Frozen Chosen or, as one of my neighbors, who struggles with three-syllable words, calls it, *Ca-na-di-a*. Considering he refers to wolves as "woofs," I take limited offense.

Recently, I celebrated my tenth year as a U.S. resident. In early 1999, I moved with my first wife and our two sons from a suburb of Toronto to a suburb of Minneapolis—from painfully cold to utterly frigid or, as some have noted, from dumb to dumber.

At the time, I held a T-1 visa, which meant the U.S. government had welcomed me with open arms to live and work in this country, just as long as (a) I didn't really plan to stay and (b) I was cool with being kicked out at any time. We purchased a spacious, beautiful home on a wooded lot, enrolled our kids in school, and with relative ease settled into both our neighborhood and our community. We even watched *Fargo* a few more times to lend our "you're darned tooteneds" a parochial accuracy. We didn't try eating lutefisk, because everyone, even those of Scandinavian descent, finds it appalling. One can only go so far to fit in.

From time to time, we would plan a visit home to Canada, each leg of which involved what felt like sixteen thousand miles of driving, dozens of hours of our cat yowling in its carrier, countless arguments in a confined space with our golden retriever adjusting its position and farting every two minutes, and several barely edible meals in Wisconsin. What exactly, I've wondered, is a chicken-fried steak? Steak? Chicken? What is it about a sirloin that really shines when it has that "chicken patty" feel? If I look hard enough through the menu, will I find a hearty tuna-poached pork chop?

On the return leg of one such trip, we arrived at the border and, because my annual visa needed to be renewed within a couple of months, stopped into the Immigration and Naturalization Service (INS) office to handle what I had been assured was routine paperwork. Routine government paperwork is about as commonplace as a gourmet, all-you-can-eat fish-fry, a successful Kentucky democrat, or a DMV worker who lives for her job.

At the desk, I presented my information with a manufactured smile and a constricted colon, fielded a couple of standard questions, and waited to receive my new card, which would replace the one currently stapled into my passport. What I received instead was a photocopy of the guidelines for visa eligibility, with one section highlighted by hand in yellow, and a note confirming I had been rejected. My mouth fell open, and my jaw settled on the counter next to a stack of brochures (each the size of a bible, with step-by-step instructions for completing the routine paperwork) and the similarly poised jaw of my first wife.

Rattled, I asked, "I'm sorry, sir, but can you tell me what this means?"

"What it means, sir . . ." Even though he fully intends to flip my world upside down with a swipe of a pen, there's no need for either of us to dispense with the niceties, is there?

". . .Is that you are no longer eligible to live or work in the U.S."

"Whoa . . .are you fucking kidding me?" This is what I wish I had said. Instead, I groveled.

"But I have a house, a job, a family, all based in Minnesota. Can you please reconsider? It would mean a lot." I almost convinced myself I could charm my way out of a crisis. For a second, I thought about a Plan B, such as asking my wife if she'd be willing to proffer a blow job to save the day, but reason prevailed. I would just sulk and hope for the best.

The immigration agent just looked at me. I thought, *Have I reached him?* His eyes said, "No, sir, you have not." Still, his face softened, and he said, "Look, I'm not an unreasonable guy . . ." My sphincter suddenly took position behind my navel, and I felt certain I was going to projectile vomit, which I doubted would help my plea. From my experience, his qualifier was like hearing "good morning" from your neighbor as he scoops dog shit off his lawn and tosses it against the side of your house.

"You can go on ahead. I'll give you ten days to settle things up in Minnesota."

Before I climbed back into our van (easier, now, because my shoulders had turned to goo), I checked my shorts to confirm I had avoided soiling myself. This was the only bright spot in what had become a uniquely glum day.

The next week and a half was a whirlwind of activity. My family arrived in Minnesota, where we unpacked and quickly repacked. We then flew back to Toronto to meet with a lawyer, drove two hours to Buffalo to resolve the issue, drove two hours back to Toronto, and then flew back to Minnesota, with new visas in hand. That was my closest brush with homelessness, even though it was also the time I had the steadiest income. Or, as my son Colin recalls, "When we were well off." Apparently, unbeknownst to me, I once had disposable income that wasn't immediately disposed of.

Just over a year later, my first wife and I divorced. There's a lot of back story I won't share here, and much misunderstanding and bitterness that still touches a nerve with many, but at the end of the process I was living in Chicago with Patty and her kids, and my ex-wife and sons were back in Canada. A year later, Patty and I were married.

There's a common misconception, reinforced by countless movies like, well, *Green Card*, that you (and Gerard Depardieu) can gain permanent resident status in the U.S. simply by marrying an American. It's not that simple . . . not at all. The process is long, exhausting, confusing, and expensive, like trying to get laid at a Christian rock concert. The expression "rode hard and put away wet" comes to mind. Actually, that expression comes to my mind often, but I'll get into that at another time.

Early in the process, you must collect reams of documents—everything from time-yellowed records of every obscure disease you've been injected against to background checks to photographs of you and your spouse doing "married people" things, like shoving food in each other's mouths while wearing matching sweatshirts or laying in bed night after night without having sex. You must have your photographs and fingerprints taken, at a designated time and in a designated place; if you miss your allotted time, you may witness two presidential elections and your second divorce before you're called again. After months and months and months of this, and hours and hours of fighting ("I thought *you* were pulling together our last twenty years of tax returns") and tears ("Why, oh why, do they need to know our preferred positions?"), you and your spouse are at last called to a final interview.

Ours was scheduled for early in the morning in downtown Chicago. We had spent the prior week collecting anything and everything we thought we might need. We had photo albums, poems I'd written for Patty ("My love for you, oh muse of mine, runs deeper than the deepest sea" . . . and such), pay stubs, even my Metropass photo I.D. for the subway in Toronto (one of my many unfortunate mullet shots). We wanted this to go off without a hitch.

But, of course, there's *always* a hitch. Our interviewer, a specialist in bad mornings, and who we guessed held records for the most consecutive hours without cracking a smile, asked for three items, none of which were on the list of suggested documents. And none of which, of course, were in the giant steamer trunk of materials we had dragged in. He said, "Look, I'm not an unreasonable man . . ." Acid flashbacks are less unsettling than this. I almost flooded myself off the hard plastic seat and under his desk near the wastebasket, where I expected my dreams to soon reside. Here we go . . .

"If you can collect one of these items, and get back to me today with it, I will approve your application."

Simple, right? If only. The next few hours included an eighty-five-minute train ride, a fifteen-minute drive to our home, a twenty-minute drive to our bank, a twenty-minute drive back from the bank, a quick break for lunch that our queasy stomachs wanted no part of, two silly arguments (both Patty's fault, as I recall), and then a two-hour drive through building traffic to return to the office mere minutes before it closed. Thankfully, though, our quest accomplished, we received the seal of approval. And something that just might have passed as a faint smile.

But the story doesn't end there. Before you receive your green card—which is, in fact, more white than green—you must still jump through a series of not-unsubstantial hoops, like a circus dog of the Pavlov school. For example, you must be endure immunizations against a number of diseases that for all intents and purposes were eradicated before the Nixon administration. It didn't matter that for the past half decade I'd traveled to seven of the largest U.S. cities and dozens of the smaller ones and, if bearing any disease, could easily have been a regular Typhoid Mary. No, before I could be made a true permanent resident, I'd have to be stuck with a bunch of unpleasant needles, one of which gave me chicken pox for the second time in my life. The bumps on my arm lasted weeks, and the scars stuck around for months. Just as the last of the bumps receded, the card arrived in the mail.

My green card—or, by its proper name, "Permanent Resident Card"—bears a photo and fingerprint of me on the front, along with a string of letters and numbers that means nothing to me but I'm sure everything to someone else. The picture is in partial profile, so it looks like I'm fact-checking the personal information to the right. On the back is the largest and shiniest magnetic strip I've ever seen, in which is embedded a faint holographic image of me and I'm sure thousands of bits of information about everywhere I've ever traveled and everything I've ever done or thought. I've wondered if my back pocket can be picked up by whatever satellite happens to be passing overhead. After all, I'm expected to have the card in my possession at all times, which isn't easy when you're among that curious breed who enjoys showers. Perhaps I can stash it with that nickel I found.

So now I'm here, probably for good. I'm a Canadian, still, but a resident of the U.S. I pay taxes, but I can't vote. That will come when I finally take steps toward becoming a U.S. citizen, which, I understand, involves pretty much going through the whole process again. ("Honey, where'd you put that picture of you and me force-feeding each other pizza?") I look forward to the day when I can join millions in dimpling a chad and watching my privilege count for nothing.

I love both my new home and the place I was born. I cheer for Canada in the Olympics, in large part because my underdog countrymen don't win a boxful of medals every day, except in curling and hockey. But I also celebrate when Americans succeed. Michael Phelps is clearly more dolphin than human; if you don't believe me, toss him a sardine and see what happens. I care about what happens in U.S. elections, both because it affects my life here and because a butterfly can't flap its wings in Washington without messing up the hair of someone in Ottawa (who will of course use this as an excuse to say Americans are terrible people). Over time, I have become a bit of an ambassador for both countries, a dispeller of misconceptions about my homeland and an eager student of my new, chosen home.

I've learned to bite my tongue when confronted with a number of odd preconceived notions about Canadians, like the prevailing belief among some that polar bears raid our garbage every week, or that we always make love doggy-style so both spouses can catch the hockey game on TV (this isn't a requirement; it's simply a preference). I offer a pinched smile when people say, "Wow, moving to the States must be like a heat wave for you," when I know from first-hand experience that downtown Chicago on a windy December day is, bar none, the coldest place on earth. And I just smile with both pride and empathy when I acknowledge the truth in my theory all Canadian men are extremely well-endowed, like we're smuggling narwhals in our BVDs. It's our oversized cross to bear.

I've fielded similar misguided questions from Canadians, who wonder why people here nickname themselves things like Chip, Buzz, and Biff (I still don't know), and who ask, with a look of incredulity, "Were there really people who thought G.W. was a good president?" The answer is yes, but most find it just as mind-boggling as you do. I've also taken exception when Canadians make blanket judgments about Americans, such as, "They never say thank you when you hold open doors for them," and, "Aren't they all heavily armed?" I explain that while this may be true in any red-colored section of the U.S. political map, most Americans say thanks, and even more feel confident they can settle differences with hand-to-hand combat.

I think of Canada and the U.S. as friends and neighbors. I don't think, as some here have suggested, that Canada is just like part of the U.S., nor do I agree when people say, "You're just the same, except you say *aboot* instead of about." There are differences, but that doesn't mean we can't revel in, and learn from, those differences. Without the U.S., Canada would never have enough good TV to fill an entire day. There's only so many adaptations of Lucy Maud Montgomery's *Anne of . . .* novels a sane person can bear. Without Canada, the U.S. would never have enjoyed Triumph, Rush, or the Barenaked Ladies (sorry about Alanis Morrisette and Bryan Adams—nobody's perfect).

Roughly three million Canadians live in the U.S., and nearly all are madly in love with both countries. If you ask us, we'll be happy to whip up a batch of poutine (French fries coated in cheese curds and gravy—it may sound vile, but everyone who tries it is hooked), watch a hockey game in any position you choose, and let you use the back of our green card to check your make-up. After all, isn't that what friends are for?

Years on the Throne

I beg of you—if you're weak of stomach, jump forward a chapter. I don't relish the idea of receiving hate mail ("Assface, I paid fifteen bucks to hear what you do in the bathroom?"), or of living with the guilt as countless dozens of you upchuck on these pages and must then buy fresh, unsullied copies of this book. Come to think of it, disregard the warning; I could use the extra royalties.

If you're of stronger stock, feel free to linger—a good litmus test is if you can watch *Trainspotting* without losing your gorge amid its celebration of bodily functions and dysfunctions (top, bottom, and sideways).

In my forty-plus years, I've endured many humiliations. The oft-rotated pimple crop on my teenaged back and face, plaid bell-bottoms with rubber boots, and being beaten senseless on multiple occasions by a girl are just a few. I've also made hundreds of truly foolish choices, including the consumption of carbonated wines with the word "baby" in their name (Baby Bear, Baby Duck, Baby Are You Going to Regret This Tomorrow), wearing a T-shirt that exposed my whole midriff (yup, guys wore these), or perming my shoulder-length hair, like Peter Frampton did before his volume of said locks and venues he played kept getting smaller.

Still, one decision that stands out from the storied pack was my agreeing to attend my first—and only—stock car race. With glee I would trade a bullet in the back of my skull for the assurance I'll never have to do it again. Sadly, on account of the enormous dimensions of my melon (not unlike a real melon or a prize-winning pumpkin), I would probably survive, only to burden my loved ones for decades in a life-long vegetative state. From my hospital bed, I would gurgle, drool, and fill thousands of adult diapers, content that I had, in a sense, still dodged a bullet.

Admittedly, I've never been much of a fan of motorsports and, from what I understand, dirt-track racing sits close to the bottom of the totem, just above demolition derbies. But I'll try anything once, most things twice, and anything eighty proof or greater as much as my fatty liver will allow.

My brother Dave and I attended such a race, years ago, as a shits-and-giggles diversion from a rainy camping weekend. The speedway, on the outskirts of a town small enough to be little more than outskirts itself, was old, broken down, and had as its only corporate sponsors the local hardware store and bakery. (Show a ticket, score a donut.) But we bought into their promotional brochure's hype about "speed and exhilaration," and even warmed up to what was billed as a "grassroots racing experience." For the uninitiated, "grassroots" is to racing what "low budget" is to film. It might be marginally entertaining, especially if you drink enough, but it will most likely suck big time.

Now, I'm not generally a snob. I could tolerate with minimal complaint the deafening racket of shredded mufflers, the blended perfume of fuel and unwashed armpits, and the incessant and inane announcements over a blown P.A. system. I didn't complain when the "high quality foods" and "comfortable grandstand seating" assailed both my stomach and my ass. I didn't even kick up a fuss at the unplanned half-time entertainment, in which a pale, skinny goof sprinted out into the middle of the field, in his altogether, and rolled like a pig in the mud. The crowd was delighted. Hey, who gets to decide what's art and what's not?

No, what turned me off such events, then and for always, was what I found when I broke from the action to answer nature's call. To feel at one both with the evening's environment and with the racing fans around me (most of whom had less couth than teeth), I stood, hitched my pants and announced to my brother, "Gotta drop a deuce." I then made my way through the throng, never once offering the courtesy of an "excuse me" to the three-hundred-pounders who had to heave their bulk to let me pass. I was in character.

Lines had formed in front of three of the four portable outhouses. The fourth, set a short distance apart from the others, was in little demand. As I opened the door, congratulating myself for my good fortune, I was shocked to find the stall occupied. No, not by Bubba, Bubbette or one of their Bublets. Instead, I was staring down the truly unexpected—a fresh, massive, and glistening mound of industrial-grade excrement. Had I spotted it in the tank below, I would have no reason to complain—and every reason to question why I felt compelled to look. No, this wasn't safely tucked out of the way, but draped proudly yet tenuously across the seat. I'd have offered kudos for the precision of placement—clearly, this was a labor of love, practically painted on the seat—but I was too busy forming my own mound, fashioned entirely of a high-quality concession stand dinner, on the grass outside. Hey, I *did* get to decide in this instance: this wasn't art.

I've shared this story at many dinner parties, usually upon delivery of the main course, and much to the delight of all. I usually follow the graphic depiction, complete with gestures, with the question, "Why do you suppose people are such pigs in the bathroom?" I then follow the quick-departing guests out of the room, asking, "Was it something I said?"

By pigs, I don't mean scumbags like the voyeuristic campers—more than one—who were arrested for public indecency when caught staring up from the holding tanks of women's outhouses. In one Canadian case, the repugnant-yet-creative perpetrator was found with a camera in one hand and a sheet of Plexiglas in the other. All together now, Ewwww. Now I bet you'll all look before you hover, won't you?

And I don't mean a former friend who, after having far too much to drink during a visit to my old apartment, found himself doing biological multi-tasking. Forced to address two imperatives at once, he threw up again and again in the sink while collecting his B.M. in wads of tissues he then unceremoniously dropped on the floor. His nightmare over, he staggered through the living room, slurred "g'night," and disappeared into my bedroom to commence the next round of the spins. I was the second to make the discovery after my brother Dave, purple from laughing, pointed at the bathroom down the hall, collapsed and mouthed, between gasps, "Nests . . . they're like little nests." If these were in fact nests, they housed the offspring of a very large—and very sick—bird. Once I could compose myself, I re-awakened this bird; I wanted no part of that.

So, if I'm not talking about bad people with their potty-cams or bad drunks who forget they've been toilet trained, of whom am I talking? For one, there's me. But not Patty. My beloved wife treats her biological imperative as a biological offense, and scrubs up after each such transgression with a zeal typically reserved for surgeons preparing to put someone under the knife. According to a recent study, only 12 percent of women leave the facilities without washing up, a sharp contrast to the full one-third of men who do so. Many times, I've tried to skulk out after a pee unnoticed, only to hear, in a voice dripping with disgust, "Get back in there. I didn't hear you wash your hands." Who listens for such things? Even if I try to fib and claim I had washed up, she won't let go. "Okay, then, explain why there's no wet spot on the sink!" I should not let this woman watch CSI. So, I guess, I am a latrine pig of sorts.

Another case in point: whenever Patty happens to walk into the bathroom while I'm peeing, my urine immediately splits into dual streams, one of which forms a large puddle on the linoleum while the other collects in the wastebasket or down the side of the shower curtain. There's no physiological rationale for this, as far as I can see; it just *is*. Just like the streaks that line the bowl whenever I or one of my sons answers the other call, but which never happens when women do their business. Why does this split along gender lines? Is there some sort of natural lubricant of which I'm unaware?

The difference between me and much of the world at large—and this is a key difference—is that I take responsibility for what I leave behind, even if I could walk away and never face the music. Not so most visitors to bars, train stations, and sports stadiums—the usual suspects—or libraries, churches, and museums, where you would think some degree of decorum might be the norm. What frustrates me is not that someone overlooks an errant drop of urine on a toilet seat, but that it's painfully evident few even try to hit what few would dispute is a decent-sized target for the task at hand. Are they just curious if the volume of their bladder is sufficient to coat a toilet, tank and all? Are they showing off for friends?

"Hey, Norm. Check this out. See, I could pee in the bowl . . ." Then a broad smile stretches across his face. "Now watch this. See how I spray my piss in all directions? Wow, I think I might have hit the ceiling on that first burst. Uh, you may want to watch your step."

These pseudo-sadists then stroll away, oblivious to the horror show they've foisted upon the next unsuspecting shmuck. It's a vicious circle, writ large, on what is supposed to be polite society.

In the aforementioned film *Trainspotting*, one of the characters visits the worst toilet in Scotland. If you've sat through this scene, nothing I've written (or could ever pen) will faze you. If you've never seen the movie, pop some corn and check it out with your kids. Few films showcase the lead character climbing into, and swimming within, a filthy toilet, all in pursuit of suppositories sprayed into said vessel moments before; the experience is uniquely poignant. Along with the disgust I felt in watching what has to be the most unsettling scene ever captured on film (with a close second awarded to a breakfast-table scene in the same movie), I felt some alarm that this room seemed not just grotesque, but familiar. I've never seen Edinburgh, but I have been in that very room, many times.

So I'd like to make a deal with you, dear reader. I will vow to attend to my business in a way that keeps it none of your business, if you will do the same. My dual streams will never wick up into your socks when you visit my home, and I'll never bring my bathroom-challenged friends to yours.

I'll even shake on it, if you'll just give me a minute to wash my hands.

Tenderness, Pleasure, Hope, and Experience

The first month of married life, according to the late Samuel Johnson, bestows upon the happy (read: ridiculously naïve) newlyweds, "nothing but tenderness and pleasure." Second marriages, to Johnson, celebrate "the triumph of hope over experience." I'm not sure how he arrived at this, since he strolled to the altar but once, but Sammy sure could crank out a sound bite. Although both quotes ring mostly true for Patty and me, our first hours were such a fresh hell it's a miracle she's still around for me to mock in print. Selfishly, Johnson stroked out two centuries ago, or we might have turned to him for advice.

Our original plan was to marry in the Catholic Church, of which Patty was a lifelong, card-carrying member. She even knows all the fancy dance moves a good Catholic makes when entering a church (kneel, dip in the water, cross yourself, jump back, do it again). However, we soon found ourselves drowning amid the flies in our ointment. ("Brian! Why are there flies in our ointment?") First, I wasn't a Catholic, and I learned I couldn't just sign up. I'm not sure about the exact protocol, but what I took from the discussions was that I would need to be belittled, reprogrammed, and purged of any Protestant tendencies if I wanted to join these vaunted ranks.

Our second problem was one of fashion. We felt a bold scarlet letter **A** might seem garish against Patty's muted silver wedding wardrobe. Patty and I had met and fallen in love before severing ties with others. I'm not proud of the hurt borne of this, but life sometimes takes sudden detours, and I knew with utter conviction I must follow my heart. Had the truth come out on *The Springer Show*, I'm sure I would have been received by a cascade of boos and censors' beeps, and some closet social worker would have wagged her finger at me and, in a shout louder than that of her compatriots, would scold, "Joo don' (beep) play folks like dat. Kick him to dah (beep) curb, honey!" Whereupon my wife would sprint off stage, wailing, with Jerry close at her heels. Backstage, he would pretend to be comforting, but would then talk her into coming back to sucker-punch me in front of thousands of the happily unemployed.

Next, we learned that what the Church of Rome had put together, the State of Illinois could not put asunder. In essence, we couldn't marry because God grants only one shot at the marriage deal; if you screw it up the first time around, tough tittie. If and when we ever get to the Pearly Gates—an unlikely prospect given the horde of skeletons rattling around in the sliver of closet space my wife could spare for me—the Lord returns us to our ex-spouses. This should be a treat for all concerned.

So, against the Pope's wishes, Patty and I settled on a more Vegas-style union.

The wedding itself was *almost* pure magic. We exchanged vows at sunset before a judge and a small audience in a moderately elegant (translation: fair but cheap) hotel suite. We had written our own vows, which necessitated that we focus on each other, so as to avoid contact with what I'm sure were a sea of rolling eyes and finger-in-throat gestures.

"You are a most exquisitely delicate chocolate éclair. Tastefully yet richly adorned on the outside, the heart of you bursts with creamy, delicious buttercream goodness." These may not have been my exact words, but they're in the ballpark.

The dress was silver and shiny (that's the best I can do; I'm a guy) and the bride looked—how do they say it—resplendent. The groom was more than a few pounds beyond svelte. For most men, the cummerbund is a decorative accessory. For me, it was a girdle, an equator delineating the upper- and lower-tier fat stores. My cummerbund (silver, to match the dress, because apparently that's important) looks in wedding photos like I'm ready to go tubing. Still, any weight issues took little away from the weightier matters at hand. We were in love, and each looked forward to our second marriages with boundless, stupid, we-won't-fuck-it-up-this-time optimism.

The first chink in the armor bore all the subtlety of being run through with a broadsword. One should not, we have learned, hire a justice-of-the-peace over the Internet. We imagined a Welsh-accented gentleman dripping in culture and refinement—imagine Pierce Brosnan in another twenty years. What we got was Elmer Fudd.

"Dee-wee be-wuvv-ed . . ."

Excuse me? In the video of our ceremony, we both look euphoric, with huge toothy smiles stretching side-to-side across our faces. In truth, we were both chomping down on our bottom lips—hard—to restrain the gales of laughter hurling against the back of our teeth. After the ceremony, more than one guest would ask, "Whoaaaa . . . What the hell was that?"

"We aww gaddewwed to witness de mawwiage of Patwicia and Bwian . . ."

Moments later, with a kiss, we joined the wanks of the gweefuwwy betwothed.

Patty's brother Neil, who managed a restaurant nearby, hosted our reception. This was convenient and bore a charming, sentimental touch. What's more, our wedding and reception cost us less than two thousand dollars—bargain basement, really, compared to the $27,000 an average wedding costs today.

I've never understood why people will pay so much for one day, when those funds could be used for something with enduring value, like a kick-ass home theatre system or a finished basement with a sport-themed bar. With close to half of first marriages imploding, many within the first eight years, that's a lot of potential car payments flushed down the toilet. Since 60 percent of second marriages go down the tubes, and usually much faster, we applauded ourselves for hedging our bets.

To say I was on a shaky footing with some of my new in-laws would be a profound understatement. Imagine the Flying Wallendas crossing dental floss between skyscrapers on ice skates with a well-armed posse blasting at them from below. Patty had been estranged from much of her family—some would have been happy to provide the needle and thread, or hammer and nails, to affix the **A** to her bosom—so our happiness in sharing our special moment was tempered by an unstable mix of awkwardness and anxiety. They clearly felt uneasy as well, because 90 percent of the photos snapped by guests at our reception were not of the bride and groom, as we had hoped, but of each other.

Less than an hour into the reception, a boneheaded remark from one guest—something along the lines of, "Aren't you thrilled your family was able to forgive you enough to be here today?"—sent Patty flying to the bathroom in tears with a dear friend, ready to make war with the antagonist, close at her heels. I was of course oblivious to this, because the four black Russians and countless shots of tequila I had employed in an effort to combat discomfort and win over my new band of brothers were now joining my filet mignon in the restaurant's dumpster. I have only the vaguest memories of swooning back to our room, and gained no popularity points with my new bride when I collapsed, crucifixion-style, across the marital bed. Patty spent our wedding night curled up on a chair. Isn't that romantic?

Patty and I have been cursed with misfortune whenever we've tried to make the most of sentimental occasions. On the night we became engaged, we enjoyed an elegant dinner, after which I proposed and, through joyful tears, she accepted. Three hours later, over drinks, I said something stupid, as only I can do with such aplomb, and Patty was hopping in a cab, alone, stopping only long enough to tell me our brief engagement was over. Now was my turn for tears. I stood on the sidewalk, blubbering and wailing. A half-hour later, after much begging, the engagement was back on, and we were both crying. We should have been taken out and summarily executed for all the overacting.

Once we got past our wedding night, we settled into the pure bliss Dr. Johnson described. Our funds were tight (a gentler way of saying less-than-non-existent), so we postponed our honeymoon for almost a year. Our timing was unfortunate. When we finally hopped on a plane bound for San Antonio to celebrate our union, tenderness and pleasure didn't make the trip.

Two legendary arguments bookended what was otherwise a fun holiday. The first was in a comedy club, of all places, and the other, even more ironically, was a free-for-all shootout of insults and salty language in front of the Alamo. Thanks to more black Russians (you'd think I'd have learned my lesson), I *don't* remember the Alamo. As Patty recalls, I was the guilty party—funny, that. Still, aside from these few setbacks, we saw eye-to-eye on enough matters to fashion an uneasy truce.

For example, we agreed that even though the eyes of everyone in a piano bar were diverted from the stage by a woman who felt compelled to repeatedly lift her shirt, our relationship would be well-served if I didn't turn around and force a third legendary showdown. (To be fair to the young lady, the evening was hot and humid.)

"Brian, don't think I can't see you straining to use your peripheral vision." I put on my best innocent face, but Patty wasn't buying it. "How tough do you suppose it would be for you to find a room in another hotel at this late hour?" For a moment, I thought about answering that San Antonio, as a popular tourist town, has many excellent facilities available, but I decided not to press my luck.

Speaking of hotels, we were also on the same page that a call to the housekeeping department was in order when our bath linens were (a) not where they were supposed to be—unless the maids' protocol was to jam damp washcloths into a corner under the sink, and (b) not in an ideal state—white linens with brown biohazard stains, regardless of how cow-like the effect, won't fly even in a cattle-loving state like Texas. I refrained from lifting the mattress off the frame to see what was underneath, as my father does whenever he stays in hotels (the last time, he uncovered a treasure trove of adult magazines, along with a sex toy whose ample dimensions are usually found only on the equine set). Patty will change rooms as readily as she'll change outfits, so I didn't want to risk a discovery that would mean repacking what had just been painstakingly unpacked.

Finally, I learned that by purchasing hundreds of dollars of gifts for Patty, taking her out for the most expensive dinner of our entire life (we gorged on fois gras without guilt, never giving a thought to the poor goose that had blown up for our benefit), and then agreeing to leave all future vacation planning to her, I would be granted a temporary stay of execution. I'm still here, so mission accomplished.

Lest I paint the wrong image, let me say that Patty is a delightful traveling companion. She's easy on the eyes, can hold her own in any conversation, laughs freely and feels comfortable engaging locals and tourists alike in witty banter. However, Patty is Patty, and she doesn't suffer fools (even the one she married) lightly.

Our second honeymoon—why celebrate something once when you can get it horribly wrong twice?—found us in sunny southern Florida. Apparently, since we live in a region known for churning out serial killers (Gacy, Dahmer, Gein, and the like), our logical vacation choices are the states most proficient at dispatching them. It also seems, by some odd coincidence, that Patty and I are inclined to choose locales sick with a phenomenon with which neither of us was familiar: feral cats.

These wild kitties are, to the uninitiated, creepy as hell. Even raccoons give them a wide berth, as we observed with some fascination from our hotel balcony. Picture *Charlotte's Web* meets *West Side Story*. Before leaving our hotel room at night, I was pressed into service as an advance scout. Only when I was sure the coast was clear—and I was certain we wouldn't walk into the middle of a feline gang war—would Patty sprint from the safety of our room to the security of our rental car.

"Wait . . . wait . . . hold . . . now . . . go, go, go!"

We spent most of our vacation in Key West. Even though the summer heat was oppressive (I had chosen July, not January, for this trek), we had a wonderful time. Wonderful, but not without stress. All of the linens were clean, to be sure; the cleaning staff was incredibly proficient, as we discovered when a maid entered our room, unannounced, to find us *in flagrante delicto*. Each time we encountered this unfortunate intruder in the days to follow, she sported an uneasy grin, which of course made me wonder if she was embarrassed by us, or *for* me, since I had chased her from our room with a certain part of my anatomy pointing her toward the exit.

I was willing to sign on for anything Patty wanted to do—shop for jewelry and knick-knacks in the many overpriced boutiques, chow on fresh seafood in upscale bistros, and pay a small fortune for a manicure and pedicure—as long as Patty would agree to help fulfill one of my dreams. I wanted to go deep-sea fishing.

I studied all the tourists' brochures, selected an option that seemed affordable and pleasant, booked a charter, and told Patty of the arrangements. I had demonstrated a degree of preparation far less than typical for me, because I wanted to make sure nothing stood between me and the fourteen-foot blue marlin I would never be allowed to mount on my family room wall. We were good to go.

"So how many bathrooms are there on the boat?"

"Honey?"

"I said, 'How many bathrooms are on the boat?'"

"Uh . . . I'm not sure." The brochure didn't have an answer. The tailfin of my marlin was disappearing into an imaginary horizon. I had hoped this was a fleeting question, and one she would forget. Uh, no.

"Don't you think you should call to find out?"

"I'm *sure* there are bathrooms." I almost believed myself.

"Call, or I'm not going."

So I called.

"Hi, yeah, hmmm . . . I'm the guy who just booked the charter. We're really looking forward to it. Umm, I have just one question: what about bathrooms?"

"What about them?"

"Well, I guess my basic question is this: are there any?"

"No."

I looked at Patty, with a feeble yet hopeful smile, and shook my head, gently. I may have even given her the "that's how things go" shrug. She too shook her head, violently. For a second, she looked like a feral cat ready to pounce.

"What would we do if, for example, my wife needed to pee?"

The phone sighed. "Same as the guys—over the side."

"Uhhh, okay, I see." Patty's head was still swinging to-and-fro, a blur, really. "You see, my wife, she's not real comfortable with all of this."

"Why not? We would all turn our heads." Now *his* phone sighed.

Like this was ever going to happen. Patty only uses public bathrooms in an emergency, and now I was going to ask her to hang her naughty bits, bait-like, over the edge of a boat and do her business in the Gulf of Mexico with not only me within earshot, but also the captain, his first mate, and any other boaters in the area? I'd have had a better chance of getting her to go backpacking in the Alaskan wilderness without a tent. So we cancelled; I have never felt less Hemingway-like. Papa would have told his woman to shut her stinking mouth and get on the boat. Papa wasn't married to Patty.

Fortunately, we later found and booked a charter with well-appointed bathrooms. I caught no marlins, but I landed two barracudas and a feisty grouper, and Patty even took the chair to snare a barracuda. We were out in the ocean for four full hours. Patty never peed once. Figures.

Our vacations have taken us to Texas once, numerous times to Wisconsin and Minnesota, and twice to Florida and Canada. All were more than a little Kafka-esque. Our second Canada vacation found our whole crew in a rustic cabin on a small lake not far from my childhood home in central Ontario. "Rustic" makes the accommodations sound much more posh than they were; the only romantic moment Patty and I shared was in alternating our attention one evening between the molded plastic "fire" and the television that received—just barely—one channel.

Our hosts were delightful people, except when they were running around the property hurling insults at each other, or when the female of the couple pulled Patty aside and wept on her shoulder. We received no discounts for providing therapy. The high point of the trip came during one of the evening group campfires (for which guests, of course, were expected to purchase the wood). While chatting with a couple who wore matching tassled leather jackets with howling wolves embroidered on the back, we discovered I had attended grade school with the husband's sister. We heard about her early adulthood, her career, and her recent marriage.

"Would you like to see pictures?"

I wanted to say, "No, never, not at all," but he was bigger and more outdoorsy looking than me, so instead I said, "Sure."

His wife ran back to their cabin and returned, moments later, with an open notebook computer. After a moment or two of fiddling, a slideshow of a wedding reception appeared on the screen. I couldn't hold back my initial reaction.

"Jesus!"

"Yeah, I know, right? Beautiful. She's just beautiful." His wife nodded vigorously. I looked at Patty, who made a gulping gesture and then looked away. "Now *you* tell me. Have you ever, in your entire life, seen more of a knockout bride?"

I can't lie—I had. I'm not sure I'd ever seen *more* bride, and I had no doubt she could *deliver* a knockout (or at least raise a nasty welt if she sunk one of her three teeth into my arm), but I have seen dozens, hundreds, perhaps even thousands of women who were easier on the eye. Never before had I so strongly believed the adage that beauty is in the eye of the beholder.

So, with our jaunts restricted thus far to North America, world travelers we are not, although Patty still fantasizes about room service in five-star hotels in exotic locales like Monaco, Florence, and Fiji. As for me, I'm still clinging to hope over experience, waiting for that moment of triumph, and ever haunted by dreams of the giant blue marlin that may one day adorn the back wall of our garage.

Funny as a Heart Attack

Sometimes, when I've rolled out one of my countless groan-inducing puns, I've expected my kids to say, "Oh, that's about as funny as a heart attack." Instead, since they're not big fans of moldy metaphors, they usually offer a simple, "Dad, shut up!" Still, in our household we've learned, through first-hand experience, that while heart attacks lack the gut-busting quality of, say, watching an annoying neighbor's house go up in flames, if you adopt a sardonic and somewhat twisted view of the world, you can see a lighter side.

On November 8, 2004, Patty arrived at school early to flit about the halls, tackling the roughly half million tasks she had cooked up the night before and that would all need to be completed to perfection before she could face students for a new term. To say she was stressed was as much as an understatement as saying, "Hitler may have had race issues," or "Men, as a rule, like sex." What's more, she was exhausted from staying up late the night before to flip the bird at the TV screen and hurl expletives each time Sean Hannity, Bill O'Reilly, or Ann Coulter appeared to discuss *Dubbya: The Sequel.*

While photocopying project lists for her new group of art students, Patty started to experience severe pain through the center of her back, across her shoulders, and down her left arm. She thought about returning to her classroom to phone for help, or heading to the office where others might be able to secure assistance. Instead, in what in retrospect seems like a shoo-in for a Darwin Awards nomination, she spent several minutes completing the copies for her class, even going so far as to reload the copier with paper for the next person. Patty is all about courtesy and decorum, even if she's a short moment away from soiling herself. Only when the pain became so unbearable that almost all her breath was stolen did she stumble to the office, where the receptionist took action that did not involve photocopying.

The phone next to my bed rang at 7:00 a.m. I employed my standard charming answer: "Coming home for sex?"

The answer was no, as expected, but I couldn't take offense since it wasn't Patty on the other end. This person sounded nothing like my wife. My ex-wife once told me Patty sounds like one of Marge Simpson's chain-smoking sisters; true, her voice is somewhat gravely, deep, and distinctive, and she is often mistaken for me, but I wouldn't go *that* far. I then heard, "You need to come here. There's a problem with Patty."

At first, I thought, *What? Did she find a sheet of paper out of place? Someone didn't push his chair in? She couldn't decide between soups of the day in the cafeteria? She saw a fly?* But I just listened, and as the details came out, I was listening less and moving more. First, I called my neighbor, because Patty had the car.

"Jim, can you give me a ride to the school? There's some problem with Patty."

"Yeah, sure. Just give me a minute and I'll meet you outside."

"Never mind, I'll just run over there." I was perhaps a trifle impatient. In a dead run, I couldn't get there faster on foot, and I'm enough out of shape that I too would require medical attention upon my arrival.

"Brian, Brian, relax. I just need to put on my pants, okay?"

I woke the kids and told them nothing other than that I had to go to the school because there was a problem. Had I shared more, Patty would be stone-cold dead before I finished answering questions. Before my neighbor's car had even come to a full stop behind a paramedic truck with its lights flashing, I was already back in motion, momentum carrying me through a red light into full-blown panic mode. I sprinted to the office, where I found Patty on the floor, topless except for a bra—a pose that might otherwise have excited me, given its public nature—with paramedics hooking her up to oxygen and force-feeding her nitroglycerin. Patty's expression terrified me.

One of the paramedics said, "Don't worry. She'll be fine. She's just having an anxiety attack." Patty looked me in the eyes and, without moving her lips, asked me, "Does this look like a fucking panic attack?" We would later read that this is a common misdiagnosis, and a primary reason women often die before they reach the hospital. Men, it would seem, can have legendary grabbers, almost as a badge or rite of passage; women, on the other hand, are prone to fits of meaningless hysteria.

I arrived at the hospital before Patty, completed paperwork with a hand so shaky I'm sure the billing department is still looking for a patient named Ptrcla OMiriCrff, and then waited for hours—actually, it was minutes, but it seemed like hours—for the ambulance to arrive. Moments later, a doctor came out, presumably to explain why my wife was suddenly a panicky person. It was the soup choices, wasn't it?

"Mr. O'Mara-Croft?" He pulled me aside, and said, "Your wife is having a massive heart attack."

I tried to rework his words in my head but, try as I might, I could not turn the word "heart," which has one syllable, into "anxiety," which no matter how fast you say it has four. I also found that my standard response when I'm nervous—to make up a filthy joke about sex—seemed as though it might be seen as either ill-timed or in poor taste. Over the next hour or so, I called anyone and everyone to share what was happening. I called friends, and left more than one terse voice message.

"Yeah, it's Brian. Hey, howya doin'? Could you call when you get a sec? Uh, Patty's heart more or less blew up in her chest. Okay, I guess that's it for now. Have a good one. Bye."

I also tried to reach most of Patty's siblings. I called my mom, so I could indulge a few minutes of unrestrained, keening waterworks. I cried hard enough to make a "wah" sound. I then called the kids, who were by then getting ready for school.

"Okay, Mom's having a bit of a problem with her heart, so just go to school and I'll be in touch, no, wait, don't go to school, just wait there until I can call again, no, maybe you should go to school, no, just stay put."

I'm sure my fumbling did nothing to allay their worries, and everything to convince them I had scattered the last few of my dwindling marbles. After what seemed like forever, a doctor came out and told me they had cleared the blockage in one of Patty's major arteries—which, because of its position and severity, is called the "Widowmaker," for the reasons implied in its catchy name. Some time later, I was brought into the ICU to see Patty.

"How are you feeling, honey?" This question made about as much sense as approaching someone who's just taken a line drive to the privates and asking, with all sincerity, "Are you okay?" But it was the best I could come up with.

"Not so well. I think I'm going to be . . ." And then she *was* sick, great streams of bile and breakfast across the front of my shirt. It was like she had saved up. Talk about a warm greeting after a tenuous absence. Dripping with vomit and sympathy, I gave her the warmest hug I've ever shared.

Patty came home five days and $50,000 later. Had this been a vacation, we would have had to indulge every hedonistic, animals-*were*-harmed-in-the-making-of-this excess known to man with twenty or more of our wildest friends to burn through so much, so fast. Thank God for health insurance.

For the first few days, Patty was so weak she couldn't mount the stairs to see the huge and still-growing mound of dishes in the sink a floor away. Gradually, though, she could move around and even insisted on supervising a number of household chores. She might have been knocking on death's door, but she wasn't going into the sweet hereafter with a messy house.

As happens to many after a heart attack, Patty developed heart failure. In simplest terms, this means her heart was no longer oblong like a football but instead round, like a soccer ball. Doctors use sports analogies so husbands can follow what they're saying. What's more, Patty's soccer ball was deflated on one side, and quivering, which would make sports, and life, somewhat more challenging.

During one of Patty's hospital stays, doctors suggested she might need a transplant, which would mean our house would need to be kept sterile at all times. I half-expected Patty to start pulling her heart out of her chest; gift horses don't trot up to one's doorstep every day. Unsettled by this news, I did what I knew had to be done: I drove into town and bought two dozen oysters and three trays of sushi. We knew Patty was going to end up on a restricted meal plan, so this was our dietary swan song. We fed ourselves, three doctors, an entire floor of nurses and a janitor, and still had leftovers.

For a while, Patty was told she could not eat fat, salt, or sugar, which meant anything palatable would be out of the question. With Thanksgiving fast approaching, though, I was determined to somehow make it special. So I found a package of vacuum-packed turkey slices that were both sodium- and fat-reduced, consulted a recipe for fat-free whole-wheat stuffing, and bought some instant potatoes I would prepare without butter. When I pulled the meal together, served it to Patty, and looked hopeful, she said, "Not bad. This really isn't bad at all." Only recently did I drag out her confession that it was the single most disgusting meal she had ever barely eaten. Only the sparkling alcohol-free wine/juice enabled her to get this abomination down. Of course, now that she's come clean about her feelings, she *looks* for opportunities to tell the story of how bad the food was. I'll have my revenge one day, though, if her condition worsens—I have grand designs on a fat-free soybean lasagna.

Patty's heart failure progressed to the point she was transferred to a large city hospital to be evaluated for a transplant. The hospital she had just left was elegant, by hospital standards, so much so that people jokingly called it a "hotel." This new place offered no such illusions. One night, Patty shared a room with a woman we have affectionately nicknamed Crack-Ho. She was dirty, smelled of alcohol, tobacco, and body odor, and had eyes that hadn't squinted upon reality in some time. Crack-Ho was admitted and, within seconds of her arrival, started wheedling her husband to take her outside for a cigarette. He resisted at first, but then relented under her barrage of profanity.

"You're a fucking loser. I hate your guts, you asshole. Take me out for a smoke, now! Fuck! Come on, you stupid dick. I need a fucking smoke. Will you take me? You will? I love you so, so much. Let's go." I found her argument, while not polished, persuasive.

After returning and being chastised for (a) leaving, and (b) smoking—both of which are frowned upon with heart patients—CrackHo settled into her bed. For less than five minutes. And then the cycle began again. Patty kept giving me the get-me-the-hell-out-of-here look, but we both knew she was stuck.

Patty was listed for a heart transplant, and assured she would get her new (actually, gently used) heart within a few weeks. She went through a battery of tests that involved invasive probing of everything from where she chews to where she poos, and had blood drawn so many times I'm pretty sure she lost weight. I was with her through many of these tests.

During the prep for one, I learned I will never again sign up to watch a urinary catheter being inserted. Some things even a perennially curious person should never see. Why does it need to be that large? In readying for another, Patty needed to be—how do I put this delicately—cleaned out. In the space of about an hour, Patty was forced to drink an enormous bottle of liquid (picture a jug of bleach from Sam's Club) which, in what has to be the cruelest joke in the history of medical product naming, was called GoLYTELY. Patty went, to be sure, but not lightly. I stood by, laughing, calling friends with the play-by-play, snapping photographs, and feeling genuine sympathy.

Among the countless routine blood tests, one, called panel reactive antibodies, or PRA, threw up a sudden hurdle.

When a person receives a transplant, the donor organ must be of a similar size, be in good condition, and both donor and recipient must have a compatible blood type. Sounds straightforward, right? Here's where the PRA comes in. Patty has off-the-charts levels of antibodies, which means that nearly every heart she received would be rejected by her body.

Whenever I pictured this rejection, I was taken back to the movie *Alien*, in which the creature bursts from one crew-member's chest. Doctors assured me that, while what I pictured was both ridiculous and a little insensitive to share, since the patient was right there, there were real dangers in transplanting Patty with an incompatible heart.

For the next several months, doctors attempted—and failed—to lower Patty's antibodies. They tried plasmapheresis, which involves drawing the blood from the body, scrubbing it in a machine that looks like it came from the set of *Lost in Space*, and then pumping it back in, sans antibodies. They tried a barrage of chemotherapy drugs, which rendered Patty hopelessly ill and incapable of eating anything but Butterfinger Blizzards from Dairy Queen. The cravings for said Blizzards arrived just minutes before the store was ready to close, and thus necessitated a harrowing seventy miles-per-hour race through suburban neighborhoods. Even if the cops were in hot pursuit, they'd have to wait until Patty had her prize before I'd let them arrest me. Still, nothing made the levels budge. We were left waiting for a heart that, barring some miracle, would never come.

When Patty wasn't sick to her stomach, or groaning from a chemo-induced headache, she slept for many hours at a time. This was preferable to staying awake, which almost immediately triggered a full-blown and enduring VomitFest. One afternoon, while Patty snoozed, her face flushed with fever, Connor looked warmly at his mother and noted in a soft tone, "Wow, it looks like she could wake up and puke at any moment."

Through this long ordeal, everyone in our home had their patience tested and nerves frayed. On a day in which Kelly was being strident, Patty snapped, "Kelly, stop being such a drama queen!" Whereupon Kelly pointed to the tubes running every which way out of Patty's chest and arm, the pill bottles that lined our dresser, and the elaborate array of pillows arranged for Patty's comfort and blurted right back, "Who's being a drama queen?"

So, Patty, never one to let anything or anyone get the better of her, just got better. Neither we nor her doctors know why she started to improve, and all still shake their heads at how well she is doing. She's not out of the woods, and never will be, but at least she no longer resembles a malevolent and unknown creature *from* the woods.

Along the way, we met an incredible number of medical professionals, all of whom could tell you in great detail what Patty looks like naked. When I nudge them, wink, and ask, "So, whaddya think?" they just offer a " Get the hell away from me, you freak" look before walking away.

Patty has had nurses who were too honest, like one who offered, "Nobody dies on the operating table. They all just waste away when they get back to their room." She visited a heart failure specialist who was easily four hundred pounds, who worked with a cardiac surgeon whose unfortunate surname is synonymous with violent murder. And she's formed strong ties with a wonderful Italian-born doctor whose personality is as flamboyant as her clothing. Dr. C, you're a lifesaver . . . really.

Patty's condition also allowed her to enjoy her fifteen minutes of fame more than once. She met the group Snow Patrol, whose lead singer kissed Patty on the cheek (a story I've heard so many times I'm sure nobody wants to hear it anymore). She chatted with Dolores O'Riordan, formerly of The Cranberries, after which I now tell anyone who'll listen, "She talked to Patty, but she smiled right at me." She even met her lifelong idol, Stevie Nicks, who gave Patty a half moon necklace that a heartbroken Patty lost while participating in a charity fashion show. Patty was the star herself at a fundraiser organized by her siblings and their spouses, at which Patty caught up with a number of friends she hadn't seen in some time. It's true—tragedy does tend to bring out the best in people.

We may not face a certain future, but who does, really? We have today, and hopefully many tomorrows. And, by miracle or perseverance, I have the old Patty back, the one that obsesses about dirt, and bugs, and how my navy blue t-shirt just won't go with my black pants. Patty will never go lightly, and I wouldn't have it any other way.

The Pursuit of Happiness . . . and Other Trivia

To say some members of our family possess a competitive streak is like saying Hugh Hefner *may* own a spacious home, and at said home one *might* find barely legal vixens with gravity-defying bosoms. Each of our crew approaches a "friendly" game of Trivial Pursuit as a rogue wolf circling a felled caribou—hackles raised, freely snarling, and baring teeth toward the hungry pack. Too often, I'm the wounded animal. My hackles just aren't what they used to be, unless you count the long, wiry hairs that mysteriously sprout from my eyebrows and ear lobes. These offend, but they fail to intimidate.

We're all in it to win. We've even known one of the boys, when trailing, to lay down his scent in an attempt to assert territorial domination. This scatters the gagging participants, and stalls the game, until the air finally clears.

"Dad! Why do you always do that? I don't want to play anymore! Mom—can you please get a divorce? Please?"

As of 2004, more than eighty-eight million copies of Trivial Pursuit had been sold worldwide. Its early and enduring success contributed to the revival of TV quiz shows like *Jeopardy*, which in turn created a fresh market for home versions (both board and online) of these TV shows. Today, you can't walk through the toy section of Target, or browse through the Web, without tripping over piles of different quiz-based games. I know. I've tripped over so many that our bedroom closet now doubles as a game-storage unit. At last count, we have more than twenty games, including four variations of Trivial Pursuit. We've bought so many games that some still bear their original cling wrap, which makes playing them a trifle more challenging and a tad less compelling.

The official name for the study and collection of trivia is "spermology" (collection of seeds, or sperma), which, on account of my XY chromosomes, makes me giggle endlessly. During one intense head-to-head game with Patty—intense only because I was being trounced and therefore acting like a brat—I complimented my wife's success with, "You're quite the sperm collector today. Aren't you, my wee spermologist?" Undaunted (and soon to be undefeated), she suggested the next time I wanted to research and throw around fifty-cent words, I should look up "eunuch" and "capon."

Once every couple of months, we gather our brood for a game as a fun way to help our kids learn new facts, since for some the mere suggestion they read a book (outside the requisite thirty-minute bedtime reading session) is greeted with the same enthusiasm as if we had suggested they save water by showering as a group. In some ways, this is a blessing, because I can pillory them on these pages with little fear our non-readers will get far enough in to become indignant or emotionally scarred.

The box for the game promises "endless hours of trivia amusement." Usually, about ten minutes in, the amusement proves *not* to be endless, and the uninhibited shit-slinging commences. The problem is that personalities—so many personalities—come into play.

There are the know-it-alls who read the card front and back and then nod sagely at what, to them, has jumped to the top of the list of most obvious questions ever. Before even letting you or anyone else in on the question, they've upped the ante by observing aloud, "This is sooooooo easy. You'd have to be an absolute moron not to get this." And I, of course, *don't* have the faintest clue and suddenly *do* have a previously undiagnosed learning disability.

Kid Two, our pack's self-appointed alpha male, routinely drives his younger siblings from the table when, in response to a question whose answer is, again, obvious, he demonstrates his spirit of fair play.

"Wrong, you stupid, fat idiot. Can you honestly tell me you're so brain-dead you don't know what team David Beckham plays for? What's wrong with you?"

Sometimes, to give the runts of our litter a fighting chance against the pack, we'll provide hints. So, while the older kids might come up with a quick answer to, "The wife of this former U.S. president challenged for the Democratic nomination in the 2008 Federal election," this question inspires only a blank stare from Kid Five. So his mother will say, "He was the president before G.W. Bush," and I'll say, "He found an unusual place to stash his cigars," whereupon Patty will yell at me for being inappropriate, again, in front of the kids.

Kids Two and Three are the arguers, certain to dispute the accuracy of answers on dozens of cards, or to turn a simple answer—Great Britain, for example—into a heated debate far beyond the scope of the game. Kid Two will say, "Most of the air battles in World War II involved American pilots standing in for the British." Kid Three will then say that, in history class, they learned that the Royal Air Force and its British-born pilots turned the tide. Kid Two will then run to my office to Google up a judge to settle the issue. Kid Three will follow, presuming Kid Two will conduct this search in an unfair way. Whereupon Kid Four, who has sat silent throughout, arms crossed and a bitter look on her face, shrieks, "Can you please both just shut up so we can get this stupid game over with?" Ah, the endless hours of trivia amusement.

I've been fortunate that while I lack a reliable or extensive long-term memory, I have instead been blessed with a healthy dose of blind shithouse luck. I once scored a key point when in response to a question about a popular deer repellent I threw the hail mary, "Not tonight, deer." (Some of the other offerings, if you face a deer epidemic in your yard, are Scoot, Deer Scram, and my favorite, I Must Garden.) Another friend once landed a pie piece when she responded to a question about a Frank Sinatra number with, "Oh, I don't know, but I bet it's something stupid." The song was "Something Stupid."

My least favorite opponents are, of course, the split-personality competitors. My friend Chris falls into this category, and for this reason I keep the trivia locked up whenever he's around. He's generous in allowing near-answers if he is so far ahead only a sudden ruptured aneurysm would keep him from prevailing. Jekyll quickly summons Hyde, though, if an opponent's sudden lucky streak presents the slightest threat to his victory. Even the reading of questions becomes laced with bile.

"Teddy bears—oh great, this is both stupid and easy—are named after the twenty-sixth president of the United States. Name him."

"Oh, I know, I know. Um, that has to be Teddy Roosevelt, right?"

"No, sorry, not right. It's *Theodore* Roosevelt. My turn."

"But that's what I meant. People did call him Teddy, after all."

"But not the people who made this game. It says Theodore, not Teddy. My turn."

As you can imagine, this particular battle quickly deteriorated. I wouldn't allow him the answer Ulysses Grant—"I'm so sorry, but you left out the S in the middle"—and threw fuel on the fire when I suggested I would make him spell Ulysses before I would relent. A later question about Pink Floyd led me to posit that while much of their music was amazing, not every song was the stuff of legend. Chris retorted by striking me on the back of the hand with a telephone handset and storming out of the room. Game over. Winner by default? Me.

If winning a trivia game at home is fun, to prevail in public is divine. These games, called pub quizzes, provide an opportunity to test your knowledge against strangers in your favorite sports bar. A question appears on the screen and you select from a series of multiple-choice answers using a funky keypad that's sticky with stale beer and wing sauce. If you know the answer immediately, you score big points, but you can salvage a few points if you quickly (and repeatedly) change your answer each time you get it wrong.

At every such bar, you'll find some bookish type who is clearly there not to drink and socialize, but to kick ass cerebral-style. He sits alone, and is easy to spot because of his expansive, shining cranium peeking out from behind a stack of nuclear physics textbooks. Then there are the middle-of-the-pack players, like yours truly and 99 percent of all other participants, who know a handful of answers and are really good at eavesdropping on other, smarter players. And then, of course, there's the person who gets more than half of the questions wrong. Smugly, you look for this loser, in the hopes you can offer a conciliatory you-can't-win-'em-all shrug of the shoulders while making sure he can't miss the smug look of superiority on your face. Unfortunately, eight-year-olds don't tend to pick up on the nuances of irony—particularly those whose parents bring them to bars.

When we were kids, we heard our parents, teachers, preachers, and others say, "It's not whether you win or lose, it's how you play the game." Richard Bach, who wrote the short-story-posing-as-complete-book *Jonathan Livingston Seagull*, once opined, "That's what learning is, after all; not whether we lose the game, but how we lose and how we've changed because of it and what we take away from it that we never had before, to apply to other games. Losing, in a curious way, is winning." Richard, let's make a bet. I'll put my pack of wolves up against your seagull in a death match any time, anywhere. There will be lessons learned, my friend. Oh yes, there will be lessons learned.

Land of the Mocking Stork

I'll be the first to admit (and Patty will quickly second this) that female logic eludes me. It's done so for as long as I can recall. Does any lad ever penetrate the psyche of his mother? Or want to? Wives and daughters too are steeped in mystery.

Ever since civilization took away early man's right to club a woman of his choosing and drag her home to do his bidding (I think this became official sometime in the late 1950s), men like yours truly have been at a total loss. So yes, I sometimes resent the so-called fairer sex, because in matters of he said, she said, they're too often right. If you doubt me, just ask them.

"I thought I made a pretty good point there," I'll say, hopefully.

"I know you do. But you didn't, really."

"But you could see my point of view, couldn't you?"

"No, not really."

"But what about the part . . ."

"No. Sorry."

"So I was just completely wrong?"

"Pretty much."

If you're a man in a more-or-less permanent relationship, a good rule of thumb is that unless your spouse tells you otherwise, you should just presume you're wrong. By adhering to this instruction, beautiful in its simplicity and resolve, you do your part to preserve an uneasy peace. In the broader scheme of things for me, though, the sum of these challenges is small potatoes, because I'm more than a husband. For some reason I can no longer recall, I also chose to be a father.

If women are tough nuts to crack, children (and teenagers, especially) are a steel-clad chest of petrified walnuts. Their thinking perplexes me more than step-by-step instructions for building a full-scale replica of the Florence Cathedral. The directions seem straightforward, but there's so many discrete pieces, and just so much work. By the time you're even close to finishing, you have to borrow someone else's hair to pull when all of your own is gone. What's more, the text is in ancient Latin—the last instruction, I believe, is *Stercus accidit* (shit happens).

Unlike with women, though, my biggest beef with children is not that they're always right—they're not—it's that they always, always, always *think* they're right. Men may be from Mars, and women from Venus, but kids must hail from some loud, twisted, and malevolent corner of the universe just a little too far out of reach of our best missiles.

In the crumbling tenements from which they must hail—reduced-scale versions of which are painstakingly recreated in their earthly bedrooms—I'm sure inane hip-hop drudge passes for music and the name Tom Petty inspires no awe. Tom freakin' Petty, people! I'm convinced these aliens invade our world only to suck the last breath of joy from life, to ask questions that inspire murderous urges ("I know I only have my learner's permit, but why can't I take the car?"), and to drain both bank accounts and refrigerators with startling efficiency.

Some mostly benign tumor—or perhaps a chip implanted back on the home planet—must encroach upon a teenage boy's developing brain. His voicebox, which until recently communicated through pubescent bleats and scratches only vaguely reminiscent of human language (if you've suffered through a twelve-year-old's choir concert, you know what I mean), has now been triggered and cannot be turned off (or down). This hidden sub-cranial growth convinces him that even though he's never paid a bill and never faced a real problem (acne or a girlfriend's mood, no matter how severe, don't really count), he can counsel his weary parents on the minutiae of life.

By turns, each of our kids has weighed in on everything from the priority of bills to Mom's inferior fashion sense (you'd have loved to be a fly on the wall for that one), to the paint colors in our family room. Could someone please beckon the mother ship?

"Dad, you're not being fair. I don't understand why you won't let me throw a party for my friends. It's *my* house, too."

Let's dissect this argument.

First, only two people in our home (and one more than the other) possess the authority to decide what's fair. Even if it's totally unfair, it's fair. In our youth, we were forced to negotiate with parents who kept us in check (or tried to), and now we're merely paying forward the odd "because I said so." Today, when I complain about the kids to my mother, do my words reach sympathetic ears? Of course not. I'm sure as soon as she sets down the phone, she relishes the long-awaited comeuppance with a loud chortle of victory and a soft-shoe step dance through her apartment.

"Vengeance is mine! Ha, ha, ha, ha. Oh yes, at long last, vengeance is mine!"

Second, I don't care if the kids don't understand; they need only accept. They don't do this very well. Too many recent books on parenting implore parents to see kids as peers or buddies—a prospect I can't abide. Real friends know how to mix a good martini, hide a corpse or proffer a blow job if your shoulders are sore. If my kids can do this, I don't want to know.

Third, this party that's never happening would require two things of me I'm forever short on—bushels of cash and worlds of patience. Listening to teenage girls talk is no less painful than repeatedly blowing an air horn directly into your ear while you claw your eyes until they pop from their sockets. How is it they don't annoy each other?

"Your bed-head looks just sick! You should keep it that way, it's dope. I hate you, bee-yotch." Giggles and screeches ensue. "Someone should call the po-po about my hair. I look so emo. Oh, snap!" A teenager would read this and say, "We don't talk like that." It's true. I was being kind; their actual conversations are far less intelligible.

Finally—and this is the big one—in no way shape or form is it *their* house. Although my kids think of themselves as princes, they are penniless paupers. Their clothes, their rooms, the hair wax with which they sculpt their faux-hawks, and even the tissue with which they wipe their tender asses are there but for the grace of Mom and Dad.

It's not always what kids say; it's also how they say it. Our children will argue with each other, to the verge of physical violence, over anything—how hot, warm, or cold it is outside, why one snack item is superior to another, when the week commences (the camps for Sunday and Monday have nearly come to blows), and even the relative amount of air each is choosing to breathe in the others' presence.

"Mom, he's bogarting my oxygen!"

This can go on for hours.

What makes this especially frustrating is the degree of hypocrisy at work. One of our sons will shriek at his younger brother for taking a prized soccer ball out on the street—"It's a Liga match ball, you stupid jerk!"—but thinks nothing of borrowing half of my worldly possessions and leaving them in the homes of his friends. Of course, he always remembers to bring his own stuff home.

Years ago, our daughter would routinely storm into our home, keening like a fire engine as she flew through the house. "Mom! Dad!" Through her great wails and gnashing of teeth, she would collect herself only enough to sob, "Uh, uhh, unhhh . . . PJ just hit me . . . unhhh, unhhh, and for no such good reason!" Whereupon we would laugh heartily at her choice of words, and the keening would resume at double the volume.

I would wager that if our family had been on the *Titanic*, our lifeboat would yield only five survivors, because by the time the kids stopped fighting about where they wanted to sit ("I'm sitting aft!" "No, you sat aft last time. Sit starboard!"), the ship and still-waiting passengers would be snugly nestled on the bottom of the ocean. Of this tragic consequence our children, still bickering, would be blissfully unaware.

I'm not sure I saw all of this coming. I always thought my children would forever adore me, and that they would regard me as heroic, all-seeing, and just plain omnipotent. Many times I recall a conversation I had at a holiday cocktail party I attended just before the birth of my first son.

To the table I shared, "I'm really looking forward to being a Dad, but I'm terrified that when my kids become teenagers, they're going to think I'm a total idiot."

Another guest at the table offered a sage nod and knowing smile; he had traveled this path, and had nuggets of wisdom to share.

"Don't worry, Brian. When they get to that age, you'll be just fine." He could see I wasn't convinced. How could he be sure? "You're missing the bigger point. You see, at the same time your kids think you're an idiot—and you're right about that, they will—it won't matter."

I asked him why.

"Because, Brian, by the time they see you as fucked in the head, the feeling will be mutual." And, with nearly two decades of parenting behind me now, I can see he was at least partially right.

Patty is much more evolved than I around the whole concept of parenting. At the same moment I'm looking under cushions to see where I left my trusty garrote—because if I don't murder the kids, I doubt they'll ever learn anything—Patty is shaking her head and chuckling.

"Brian, they're just being teenagers. That's what teens do."

"You're telling me that teens' selfish, thoughtless, illogical behavior is just a function of what—their wiring?"

"That's what I'm saying."

"I'm leaving you."

"No, you're not. I'd eat your lunch."

So I've resigned myself to the idea that I may not like the way kids work but, since I can't flee, I need to make a better effort to understand. I read somewhere that one way to achieve greater appreciation of your children is to participate in activities important to them. So, just the other night, Patty and I chaperoned a homecoming bonfire at the high school at which she teaches two of our kids.

This event promised one of my favorite things, a barely controlled conflagration, and one of my least, spending an evening in the presence of unbridled hormones (this too a barely controlled conflagration). Scratch that: unbridled hormones are good—just not in children. We chaperones were each deputized for our role, equipped with a flashlight, and given clear instructions to intercept any questionable behavior, particularly "juking."

To my surprise, it turns out juking does not involve popping in a quarter and choosing three songs. Instead, it's basically dry humping before a cheering throng. If I understand the process, and I'm not sure I want to, a girl grinds her hindquarters provocatively against a boy's crotch to music while he grasps her hips and grinds back. When I first saw this in the flesh, I was lost. My first instinct was to grab a water bottle and extinguish the blaze. My second was to run as fast as I could and not stop until I crossed the Canadian border. There is something unsettling about seeing kids behaving as sexual beings, especially when your daughter is unaccounted for somewhere in the crowd. What I did know, with absolute certainty, was that I wasn't going to break things up by pushing through the middle; to use a bad pun, I had no desire to be the butt of someone's *juke*.

Before the bonfire wrapped up, I spotted a couple whose cuddling was getting too cuddly for my taste. My flashlight shot up above my head like a Jedi light saber. I was readying to push the button when my arm was knocked from the air.

"No, Dad," my daughter pleaded. "What they're doing isn't juking. It's okay."

"You think *that's* okay? He looks like he's hot-glued to her back."

"No, what they're doing is fine."

Wow, good thing my daughter tried to save me from embarrassment. Too bad I didn't save her. I hit the switch, and my light went through the quickly separating couple. Just as rapidly, my daughter vanished. Later, I explained that, for her, cuddling in that fashion was in no way fine and, unless she wanted police to troll local lakes for the offending boy, she had better chop off the hands of anyone who got too eager.

Sometimes, though, kids do cross lines, and responsible parents owe it to themselves and their children to bring the hammer down. Patty holds strong opinions about how to mete out parental justice. Come to think of it, I'm not sure there's anything in the entire universe about which Patty doesn't have a strong opinion. Again, I don't understand the logic, and I'm told this is okay. Problems arise when I find myself trying to interpret and then enforce the Code of Mom.

Here's the rub. I want to police the rules my wife has devised. As a guy, I want to be powerful and intimidating. Who better than your kids to bully? Try as I might to play the heavy, though, I'm a bit of a wimp. I forever fall into one of two modes. Mode One is wishy-washiness. In an angry tone (and from another room, so I don't have to make eye contact), I take something away. Minutes later, I find myself consumed with second thoughts, and hours later give in completely. The kids simply wait me out. Mode Two involves devising over-the-top punishments for offenses big or small.

"You said you would be home by eleven. As you can clearly see, it's now three past eleven. So, for each minute you were late, you will spend a full month in your room—no telephone, no television, no conversations with your siblings through the door. You are a non-being. You may take a short bathroom break twice a day, and shower when I determine you smell foul. I still haven't decided whether or not we'll feed you. And you'll be *happy* about all of this."

When Patty questions the fairness of my verdict by saying, "When did you become a hero among morons?" I find myself wondering why she isn't being more supportive of one merely defending her principles and honor. To date, I haven't kept the kids grounded for even a single month. How fair is that?

Where we differ, and where most men and women deviate, is in our macro view of the whole area of discipline. For men, these decisions are black and white. The only color is in the language we use—"Kids, these are the rules; if you slip off the beaten path, it's lethal injection for the lot of you." Women, by contrast, are comfortable navigating through the grayest of gray areas.

I may never get the hang of this parenting thing. By the time I do, I suspect I'll face the specter of grandchildren, for which I'll be even less prepared. I guess I'll just toe the line, follow orders, and try not to sentence my kids to life terms—all for no such good reason.

Straining the Weakest Link

"Earth has its boundaries, but human stupidity is limitless." So spoke Gustave Flaubert, the French realist writer whose greatest successes included (a) no Mrs. Flaubert, and (b) penning the novel *Madame Bovary*. I've never read the book but, from its title, I picture tuxedo-clad cows, harmonizing vaginas, and loveless sex for hire. In other words, I picture my better dreams.

Flaubert's less auspicious accomplishments include (c) never meeting a venereal disease he didn't like, (d) bearing an uncanny resemblance to a heartbroken or syphilis-plagued walrus, (e) spending most of his life either with prostitutes or his mother and (f) wasting the boundless merchandising potential of his name. So readily he could have named a cheese after himself, as in "I'll have the tawny port with artisan crackers and hmm . . . how about a creamy Flaubert?" Or he could have introduced a novel cooking technique: "The poached salmon sounds divine; but could you trouble the chef to serve it Flauberted?"

The author's sunny observation about our collective lack of common sense may well have faded into obscurity were our world not still overflowing with stupid people. Web sites and reality-TV programs celebrate those who have taken idiocy to a whole new level. I look for these shows and these sites; these are my people.

My people do not include contestants on *Fear Factor*. The

twits who end up here go beyond stupid to a transcendent state I call "fucking idiotic." I would not compete to be the fastest to down a mold-covered sheep's penis crawling with maggots, even if I could score $50,000 for "winning." In fact, you could say to me, "Here, Brian. Fifty thousand dollars. Just eat the penis." I couldn't do it. I'm not anti-penis, per se; I'm just not evolved enough to regard it as a "foodstuff."

On one Web site I read about a twenty-nine-year-old Florida man who, after being denied sex, drew a pistol and blasted himself twice in the arm. Why? If I maimed myself every time I received the cold shoulder, I'd be a hobbling, blood-soaked 220-pound slab of Swiss cheese. This assumes, of course, I'd have the stamina, blood supply, and surface area to withstand hundreds upon hundreds of gunshot wounds each year.

"Patty. Psst, Patty." I shake her, just a little, enough to make her head snap all the way forward and back. "Hey . . . hey, Patty."

"Nnnnggh." This is sleep-talk for everything from the sound itself, to more complete thoughts, like *fuck right off*. She's moving away from me in the bed, but has left an aura of menace where her form had been. The aura is awake and glaring at me. It looks like a very, very large and threatening Siamese cat, and a little like Margaret Cho.

"Patty. Patty." I'm not sure, but I think she smiled. If I play my cards right . . .

"Patty!"

A nightmare—it must have been—because now she's bolt upright. I think she's showing off, what with the panting and violent twisting of my index fingers, the same fingers that a second before I had jammed into her ribs.

"What?" I don't much care for her tone. It's harsh and, to be honest, a little hurtful. It's killing the mood. "Brian, what?"

I want her to see she's wounded me. "It's nothing." I pause for effect: one, two, three. "Go back to sleep."

But now she won't let it go. Forced now to speak my mind, I ask, "You wanna?" I even cup one of her breasts, because I read somewhere that women really dig that, especially if you turn the nipple like it's a volume control. It works; the next time she speaks her voice is louder.

"Are you kidding me? No."

"Please?" Good move, Brian. Kill her with kindness.

"No."

"I'm sorry . . ." I'm still not certain if I've heard her clearly. Did she say no, or certainly?

"Did you just say no?"

"Yes."

"Yes to sex, or yes to no?"

"No."

I'm devastated now. I don't know whether to slap myself (stupid, stupid, stupid) or beg (please, please, please).

"Please?"

"No."

"Patty, please?" Another nice touch; personalize the message. Why isn't it working, huh, stupid, stupid, stupid? I try another tack, as a last resort, before grabbing my bottle of roofies.

"You leave me no choice. Either we make love right now or, so help me God, the arm gets it."

"No."

"No to shooting myself, or no to sex?"

If every male followed my Florida friend's M.O., we'd all wander around with dead arms flapping by our sides, like those duck lawn ornaments with the spinning wings (which, of course, look nothing like real ducks, but more like meth addicts in duck costumes). Never again would we see a football play celebrated with a spiked ball in the end zone and a resounding low five on the ass. (Does anyone, anywhere, understand why this happens? I don't go to my doctor, suffer through an invasive examination, accept a prescription, and then grab a fistful of my physician's buttocks while shouting, "Good one, doc!" Nobody gives me a reach-around if I pick up their mail while they're away for the week. And yet, as I write this, I wonder if more ass slapping might not make us all better friends. I'll do some research and get back to you.)

If our gunshot victim had smarts, he wouldn't have taken out his frustration on his own limb. Where I come from we call this "counterproductive" or, sometimes, "masturbation-limiting." No, had he used his noggin, he would have flipped the gun the opposite way—gun stock toward shooter, gun barrel toward shootee—and let her have it. Don't get me wrong: I'm not subborning violence against women. And I'm speaking only of a grazing wound—a hint, really. But what he could have achieved by shooting her—an incentive for change—is different from what he actually accomplished, which was to make him seem almost unbearably *needy*. Let's face it, nobody finds that attractive.

When we read about stupid acts, we view them as isolated incidents, and pat ourselves on the back for exercising superior judgment. And yet, as a supposedly civilized society, we still have laws on the books that defy logic. In my home state of Illinois, it's against the law to offer lighted cigars to pets. This hasn't presented much of a problem in our home, where most of our animals have been non-smokers and, were they not, I would always have thought them to prefer cigarettes.

In Pennsylvania, homeowners cannot hide dirt or dust under a rug in their dwelling. I've never shared this story with Patty because I'm certain she'd press legislators in our state to follow suit. Soon, people would be caned for failing to put the toaster away after use, and leaving an empty soda can on the coffee table would be a capital offense.

My favorite, though, comes from Alaska. In the far north, you can find yourself in hot water if, just for yuks, you shove a moose out of an airplane. I didn't see the actual statute, so I imagine there may be exceptions made for (a) skydiving or (b) self-defense. I will tell you this: If I'm flying to Anchorage on a book tour and, as I approach the bathroom, I stare down a charging bull emerging from first class, I'm sorry—it's him or me. And yet, as I picture myself jettisoning this moose, I can't help but think of later consequences. I'm haunted by a picture of some unfortunate sap who steps outside his cabin to grab the newspaper, checks the sky for coming rainclouds, and instead loses his share of sunlight to a moose-shaped shadow of rapidly expanding proportions. Now imagine what the moose thinks. It's all so convoluted, so I guess this law is a good one.

But not all laws are good ones. Some of the more stupid ones are dead serious. Our lawmakers administer little more than a slap on the hand to people so inebriated they drive a riding lawnmower, scooter, or favorite milking-horse to the liquor store when we've taken their licenses away, yet they think nothing of tossing someone in prison forever for smoking just enough marijuana to take the edge off our cocaine, or to make a visit from in-laws tolerable. It seems a strange and unfair irony that we're filling our joints for, well, joints.

I'll admit I've experimented with marijuana, but no more than, say, a thousand times. I don't believe in letting anything get out of hand. I will admit, though, that I inhaled, not because I've never aspired to a career in politics, but because smoking pot is worse than pointless if the smoke doesn't make it to your lungs; what the fuck is wrong with people? But, just because when I do things,

I like to do them right, does this make me a criminal? Should I be punished for an indulgence that at its worst results only in my walking to the store for a family-sized bag of chips, a container of French onion dip, three shrink-wrapped cheeseburgers, one quart each of regular and chocolate milk, a tub of rocky road ice cream, a bag of salted peanuts, and four packets of brown mustard I'm stealing in the hopes I'll find something in the fridge or pantry at home to dress them with? I shouldn't be punished. I should be lauded for stimulating the economy—especially when I finish the lot and then order a family-size meat lovers' pizza.

Lest you think I'm being too hasty in casting the first stone at stupid people, I should share my own brush with personal extinction. There are several, but for now I'll share just one.

Like all men, I love fires, and the bigger, the better. As a Boy Scouts dropout, though, I never mastered the bow-drill method of fire creation. Nor have I figured out how to start a fire with a magnifying glass without suffering temporary blindness when, to torment myself, I redirect the light into my eyes. So instead, in the interests of efficiency, I employ accelerants. In our backyard fire pit I will stack wood either in a log-cabin or tepee configuration (I've picked up that much along the way), douse the works with at least a half-bottle of lighter fluid and then lob a lighted match from a safe distance (through trial, error, and the loss of most of my body hair, I'd guess this to be around twenty yards). Voila—instant ambience! I will then apply liberal squirts of liquid until I am certain the wood itself is burning, and not just the fuel upon it. This can take as many as four containers of fluid; the key is to believe in your fire-crafting talent and to stay the course.

One evening, my brother-in-law Neil was helping me to start a fire for an evening cookout. The firewood had been rained upon, and even a case of lighter fluid was making little difference, so we were faced with limited options. We could steal and burn the neighbors' picnic table and, depending on how late we wanted to stay up, their deck. We could start a fire in the fireplace inside, and then carefully lug the burning pieces through the house and out the back door. Or we could find something that could render wood from a slow-starter into something gently explosive. This had some appeal. We tried a bottle of torch oil. Yawn. And then Neil remembered how, on a previous occasion, Patty had tossed spent tealights into the firepit, and that the residual wax had flared up, adding brief intensity to the fire. Neil excels at math and science, so when he suggested that if a tealight added brief intensity, the citronella pail sitting on the outdoor bar could also perk things up, I was in no position to argue.

The conflagration was Biblical. Our gentle nudge within seconds became a fair replica of the Gates of Hell. Flames shot twelve feet into the sky, and were climbing at a steady pace. Any low-flying planes would soon need to alter flight paths or risk charring their landing gear. What's more, a gentle breeze was now bending this inferno, like Beckham, ominously toward our vinyl siding. Neil and I agreed that if Patty popped her head outside to find a fire bigger than anything seen in the oil fields of Kuwait, along with the entire back of our home engulfed in lapping, waxy flames, she may well become surly.

And then, dear reader, things started to go bad.

Today's lesson: if you've built a fire more than twice your height and as big around as your kitchen table, and have added highly flammable materials to said fire, do not—and I can't emphasize it enough when I say *do not*—spray it with a blast of icy water from a garden hose. We, of course, did. Anyone whose yard faced ours was treated to their first-ever mushroom cloud, a mini-Hiroshima in the heart of the American Midwest. The concussion was astounding. If you imagine the letters before you as a normal speaking voice, you must picture this particular whoomp in three-hundred-point bold type with twelve to fifteen exclamation points at the end.

In the immediate confusion, and through the enormous bales of smoke and heat radiation, I couldn't spot Neil. Had he been vaporized? Was he clinging for dear life to the peak of our roof? Would I find him in a crumpled, distorted heap in our neighbor's backyard? As I screamed his name, everything moved in slow motion, like in one of your better war movies.

"Neeeeeeeiiiiillll!"

The smoke cleared enough to reveal Neil. He was alive, largely unharmed and intact on the other side of the fire pit, hugging the ground and looking like he couldn't decide whether to sob or laugh hysterically. He opted for the latter and then I, knowing a negligent homicide rap wasn't in my immediate future, laughed as well. Patty arrived at the patio door, assessed the situation in a split second, and immediately adopted her favorite "what the flying fuck did the two of you do now?" glare. She wasn't so much concerned about injury as she was about public humiliation. A driver from two streets over screamed around the corners between where he was and where we were and ran out to ask us if we were okay. Then he asked if we were out of our minds.

We waited to hear sirens, but they never came. For at least a half hour, we wouldn't have heard them anyway, because we were more or less deaf. This turned out to be a blessing in disguise, because when Patty unloaded on us we were mostly spared; I did lip-read "asshole" and "trial separation" more than once, but much of her rant looked like an impersonation of a largemouth bass closing in on a lure. Funny, to be sure, but we dared not laugh. The impact of her tirade was lost, as was the evening cookout.

So are we all idiots at times? Is it human nature to engage in behaviors that are foolish and self-destructive? When my brother Dave was run over by a car while walking through a McDonald's drive-thru, was he living on borrowed time? Or was he just too non-conformist to have accepted "drive-thru" as a literal definition? And what of my ex-wife, who while driving in a manner she considered safe, has been struck by both a school bus and a large horse? Even Patty, the champion of good sense, laid her hand wide open while scooping wax with a sharp knife from a glass votive holder and, when we met, sported a bandage to hide the damage she incurred when she jammed her finger into a fan. Why are we so free to set reason aside?

Modern man has by no means cornered the market on foolish. It would seem we've been dumb since Eve became the first person to sample fruit before paying for it (and, oh, did she pay). If I had been Adam, Eve would have been oblivious to forbidden apples, because I would be forever guiding her toward other forbidden fruit. "Hey, Eve. Stop looking around you, I'm talking to you. Yes, you. You are the only other one here, you know." Then I'd compliment her on her outfit; few bathing suits are fashioned from a single fig leaf anymore. Then I'd gulp down another mushroom cap from the Garden, just so I could hear the snake talk again. A few generations later, I'd be there again, suggesting to Noah that perhaps he could exclude mosquitoes, spiders, cockroaches, cats and right-wing politicians from the passenger list. But no, we started stupid and, it would seem, carried on this proud tradition.

So perhaps it is human nature to laugh in the face of danger and possible death. Or it may well be I have no business commenting on the stupidity of others when I'm so proficient at demonstrating it myself. I do know I will never eat an eyeball on

TV (unless it's hidden with the snouts and hooves in a hot dog), nor will I push a moose out of an airplane. For one, I have neither a spare plane nor a spare moose. And besides, that would just be plain stupid.

Favor of the Month

"Brian, I need a big favor."

I'm a big-favor kind of guy—I happily giveth and taketh away kind acts. I'll be the first to accept others' altruism. "Hey, Joe, grab the other end of this black zippered sack, would you? We just need to drag him . . . Did I just say 'him'? Ha ha ha . . .I meant 'it,' to the backyard." This world is chock-full of such complex challenges and moral ambiguities, and to negotiate such turbulent seas one needs friends. So, if without hesitation I'll rely upon others' kindness (and corpse-stashing talents), I'd have to be a self-absorbed jerk not to entertain their simple pleas.

So when my neighbor asked for a favor, my only choice was to ask: how could I be of service? A cup of sugar? A fifth of Ketel One in a brown paper sack? My first born in my next life? (Presuming, of course, I'd be insane enough to revisit that fresh hell.) A list of referrals to have someone whacked?

"How do you feel about running to the sex toy store for me?"

Tada! At some point in their lives, don't all guys answer the call of a married female beseeching us to purchase adult material on her behalf? With few sacred cows amid my herd, this was an easy yes. For some, it would not be. I could not, for example, say to my mother, "Hey, Mom, are you still planning to run out to Yarn Barn this morning? Any chance you could swing by Smut Hut and grab me a pulsating lifelife vagina?" Her answer, I am sure, would be no. Besides, what if she said yes, and then got there and found more than one model to choose from? Walking through the features of each option would be more than a little awkward. "Well, Mom, of course I want the variable speed control. No, I don't need the vaginal extension." I also know with certainty my wife will never make a similar request. "Brian, go pick something. Surprise me!"

My mission this time was, by porn store standards, tame—grab something nice yet tasteful for a bachelorette party. This is no small feat in a store that peddles chocolate penises on sticks and the equivalent of a Big Mouth Billy Bass with the fish replaced with boobs. Immediately, my mind flooded with great ideas.

"Oh, I know, I know. I've got it. We'll set her up with the Master Violator Max IV, a twelve-pack of AA batteries and the optional Power Blast AC adaptor. Oh, and maybe a black leather pleasure swing. Yeah, all of that, and we'll get her a riding crop. They're doing great things in the S & M market these days."

My enthusiasm, though fairly screaming, fell upon deaf ears. My damsel in distress was not even on the same page. Had I pursued my description of the various options, I'm certain she would have dropped the phone, plugged her ears, and did a "La, la, la, la, I can't hear you," just to drown me out. I left well enough alone.

She proposed not a colossal prosthetic, nor any flavor of edible garment (strawberry, cherry, orange, spicy brown mustard, penne à la vodka). Instead, I was tasked to find nothing more than a sexy book. I was going to what was called (ambitiously) an adult superstore and would come away with a mere book? They sell sex-themed books at Barnes & Noble! True, you can't peruse this modest selection at length without looking like a pervert, someone whose time would be better spent at the adult superstore, but still you can find a spicy tome there. In the sex shop, if you weren't at least a little twisted, you wouldn't be there; everyone's a pervert, but it's relative. So only a book? Yawn.

My first instinct was to say, "Either we do it my way, chickypoo, or the deal's off," but then I recalled the many times her husband saved my bacon (and perhaps my marriage) when we needed an emergency household repair. Even as I wrote this chapter, we pressed him into service to unclog a nasty drain. At first, I thought I could fix it myself. However, after looking at the drain for a considerable stretch, hoping the problem would resolve itself amid my Kreskin-style fierce concentration, Patty said, "Are you kidding me?" and picked up the phone to call in reinforcements. These friends have helped us out so many times I could turn down few requests short of smuggling a dozen condoms stuffed with heroin into the country via my rectum. Even that I'd have to ponder, but would haggle on the number; I've never checked, but I suspect it's snug back there. So, if a book this housewife wanted, a book she'd get.

By some good fortune, I've been sitting on a veritable Library of "Congress", a shelf of shamelessness, tucked away (I hope) from prying eyes. Purchased in the early days when just locking the bedroom door unlocked a world of bawdy adventure, they now collect dust next to the fur-lined handcuffs and glow-in-the-dark bath bubbles. All of these seemed like spectacular ideas at the time—except for the fluorescent body paint, the packaging for which warned any oral contact might result in poisoning. Given the faint likelihood of my ever again dipping into my supply of carnal playbooks for ideas, I should have trashed them. You can't easily give naughty books away, or box them up for a church rummage sale. I suspect even our local library, which accepts donations with open arms, would opt against adding *Become a Cunning Linguist* to its collection.

On this occasion, however, I found a friendly consumer willing to take a few of the tamer texts off my hands. My books were in pristine condition (from utter lack of use), so I suggested my neighbor pick two or three titles and re-gift them. Perhaps they would open doors for others that, after years of marriage, are forever closed to me. What's more, I would still score points for being willing to go, without actually making the trip in pursuit of a stupid book.

It seems I'm always willing (or foolish enough) to entertain ideas on society's fringe. I won't give a hand job to a Shetland pony no matter how cute it is, but I will engage in activities at which others would balk. As a teenager, I turned my brother's overactive libido, and my good fortune in looking older than my fifteen years, into a lucrative under-the-radar business. I would purchase nudie magazines from the local pharmacy in exchange for a five-buck-per-volume fee and, of course, a cursory preview of the material. Dave had no qualms about reading the foulest smut ever dreamed up by humans, and in copious amounts, but had real issues with being seen doing so. I had no qualms about anything, especially for a price. We call this "symbiosis."

When I met Patty, I already had some explaining to do for the choices I made in the decades before our meeting. In particular, she took issue with my predisposition toward public nudity. For years, the mere mention of skinny dipping caused me to scatter my clothes and lead the charge (Banzai!) toward the beach, usually alone. During one hot-tub party in a neighbor's yard, I retrieved a six-pack of beer from my fridge across the street, without bothering to don my swim trunks before doing so.

"Brian, I think you're missing the point," Patty told me. "No, scratch that. You *are* missing the point. Why were you naked in the hot tub to begin with? With the neighbors? *And* where, pray tell, were the kids?"

Now how can I even answer her charges? I was too warm? I was worried the chemicals in the water would fade the fabric of my trunks? I buckled under peer pressure? Truth be told, I don't even know why I was naked; it just seemed like the right and natural thing to do at the time. Besides, the kids were in bed before I even shed my shorts; now who will dare call me an irresponsible parent?

Even when I told Patty, hopefully, that I employed the six-pack to cover my immodest behavior on the return trip, she wasn't charmed. She didn't do things like this. She did nothing even remotely like this—ever. So imagine my pleasant surprise when I once cajoled her into accompanying me on a visit to the adult store. This lasted about six seconds. When she heard one employee say to another, "Hour's up. It's your turn to disinfect the bathroom again," Patty made an abrupt turn toward the door. She hasn't been back. I don't rattle so easily; I just pee before I leave the house.

From time to time, for pure scientific research, I still make the trek in an attempt to understand what inspires today's young folks. The particular nondescript building at the side of a freeway bears a name that brings to mind a luxury cruise ship. Any suggestion of a cruise-ship theme disappears the second one walks through the door.

What surprises and alarms me (yes, even me) is that these stores stay open twenty-four hours a day, seven days a week, and never seem wanting for customers. Is the need for such materials—ironically called "marital aids"—so strong that people must have unfettered access, day and night? Who out there has a 3 a.m. craving for a nubby butt plug? Don't answer. And yet, while it would seem many marriages are in need of desperate aid, a quick scan of the patrons reveals few one would consider the proverbial marrying type.

If you've never wandered into one of these places, let me share what to expect. First, if you're a guy, expect to pay a deposit (called a browsing fee) to walk through the door. The reason is obvious: the owners don't want horny men living amid the racks of magazines.

"George. George! Set the November issue of *MegaJuggs* aside for a minute, you fiend. The delivery guy's here with your pizza. And move that damned sleeping bag over; you're not the only one here, you know!"

To get your deposit back, you must buy something. A safe first purchase is a flavored lubricant or fancy condom (perhaps peach-flavored, if you're feeling especially racy). A gutsy purchase is a full-scale replica of a disembodied torso or a head whose mouth registers permanent surprise. Women, who with few exceptions want to get in and out with haste, get in and out for free. Face it, though. This isn't the place to meet chicks.

The next thing you should know is that no matter what your variety of kink, as long as it's legal, you'll find something that caters to it, especially in the video section. Are you a fan of hunchbacked little people? Hefty middle-aged women who clearly fear razors? Balding, frustrated accountants? (No wait, those are the customers.) Oversexed members of the medical profession? Armenian sheepherders dating one-legged grandmothers? You're in the right place. The U.S. adult film industry churns out between four and eleven thousand films each year, which translates into up to thirteen billion dollars in gross revenues. Some of these revenues, clearly, are unspeakably gross. But at least the industry keeps hundreds of Americans gainfully employed.

The walls of my local store, festooned with hundreds upon hundreds of "toys" bearing a great or only passing resemblance to anatomically correct human parts, forever put to rest the argument "size doesn't matter." Women who have fantasized about Tom Thumb, Mister Ed, and all historical figures in between, need only reach up to find their prayers answered. My favorite is the rubber arm complete with closed fist; I presume this is to defend yourself if someone tries to steal your toys, or to drape over your wife's shoulders after lovemaking to fool her into thinking you're cuddling. I won't delve into specifics about everything on these walls, but let's just say that the whole section would humble the average man.

If toys aren't your thing, you can instead shop for games, lingerie (which nobody tries on, since the fitting room is the aforementioned bathroom), lubricants, magazines (in shrink-wrapped two packs, for better value), weekly newspapers, and pills or lotions that promise to render mere mortals into long-lasting lotharios. Unless you possess a uniquely creepy imagination, or you're the one that stocks the shelves, you're sure to be surprised more than once at the offerings. Even I was.

What makes a mere adult store into a superstore, I would guess, is not the selection of products. You'll find more items, overall, in almost any boutique. But most boutiques don't boast a movieplex tacked on the back. No Spike Lee joints or Hitchcockian revivals play these screens. No, beyond the beaded curtain you'll find only features that require tokens to be fed in, one after another, to keep the film running—sort of a Chuck E. Cheese for the morally bankrupt. None of this would be unsettling were it not for the cascades of orgasmic shrieks and moans that stream out of the back room and into the store proper. Any attempt to be discreet in your purpose—to the extent anything can be discreet when you're flipping through pictures of spread-eagled women in the presence of others—goes out the window when, "Oh, yes, Daddy. Yes!" flies past your head. If I'm ever there and someone taps me on the shoulder, I plan to pretend I've been sleepwalking. "How the heck did I end up in here?" Then I'll claim the moral high ground. "And what are you doing here?"

Lest I paint myself to be a complete reprobate, I should say I'm not a regular customer. I don't walk through the door with my browsing fee in hand, only to have the clerk wave his hand and say, "You're good." Nobody greets me by name, or asks me if I want the usual. I don't have a line of credit, or an affinity credit card emblazoned with the company's logo. I don't plan my evenings around a visit to the store followed by an hourly rental at one of the seedy motels just down the street. No, I'm not that kind of guy. I'm just your big-favor kind of guy, doing my small part to bring happiness from afar to brides-to-be everywhere.

Not a Guy's Guy

As I flip through *Men's Journal* each month, dabbing bitter tears from my eyes and choosing recipients-to-be for anonymous threatening letters, I rehearse countless "if onlys."

If only the Testosterone Fairy had distributed his gifts fairly, instead of bestowing great fistfuls of manliness upon others and shaking scant crumbs from the bottom of the box for me. If only I could have been the quarterback, the valedictorian, the gigolo, the member of The Village People—roles only for the most unambiguously masculine and virile of young men. If only I could hear from women, "Oh, I wish my husband was more like you," without also having my male drinking buddies lament, "Oh, I wish my wife was more like you." If only I could face my fears without running at a full sprint in the opposite direction, all the while shrieking like a flame-engulfed Richard Simmons.

Unfortunately, I can yearn for as much hair-raising adventure as *Men's Journal*, *Backpacker*, *Outside*, and *Penthouse Forum* can dream up, but my reality will always be more sedate and uninspiring. I could never create detailed schematics for *Popular Mechanics*, or even read the magazine without breaking out in hives. And yet, most weeks, I could tell you which store has the best deal on tampons.

I'm never the one invited to bow-hunt charging herds of

water buffalo, but I can identify gabardine more readily than any outdoorsman. I'll never lead the first expedition to scale Kilimanjaro backwards, but I have a pretty good idea of what a menstrual cramp must feel like.

And I doubt I'll ever achieve more than 88 percent success in using just my mind and the second knuckle of my ring finger to bring a woman to new heights of pleasure (the 12 percent failure rate due mostly to my fear of heights). But, with just my mind and the second knuckle . . . well, you figure it out.

Try as I might, I'll never be your classic guy's guy. I may want to sleep on an aluminum and fabric portaledge 2,700 feet straight up the side of Yosemite Park's El Capitan, but I'm too restless a sleeper. On a bed, tossing and turning is okay. On a platform hundreds of feet in the air, not so much. I'm not up for the gamble.

Stand-up river paddling through raging whitewater looks fun, but all of my attempts to swim so far have elicited either laughter or sympathy. The alternative, drowning, has never appealed. Fighter pilot for a day? Fine . . . until I crash.

I'd much prefer something where the risk and reward are more balanced. If I can enjoy myself, feel naughty and outrageous, and have no risk of drowning, that's more to my taste. That's why, while all the other guys battle waves, I'll be dangling from the hanger bar on my wife's side of the closet, masturbating like there's no tomorrow.

The simple reality is that I lack confidence (along with skill, physical attractiveness, charm, smarts, and countless other qualities that distinguish, say, Johnny Depp from, well, everyone else). As much as I aspire to be like John Wayne in his prime, I suspect even Carson Kressley (of *Queer Eye* fame) could easily beat my ass all over the room. I am a guy. I'm just not the kind of guy parents and friends call Duke, or Biff, or Jean-Claude. More than once, I've been mistaken for someone named "Faggot," but

I'm pretty sure we've never met.

So, as I read my magazine, I wondered if I'd find anything at all for someone like me. I had almost given up hope when I hit an article about Quarterback Camp. I read a few of the prerequisites and, although I was not an ideal candidate, I thought I could perhaps fake my way through. How tough could it be? I think I could take a snap without dropping it. If I wasn't under too much pressure, I could look for, and find, an open receiver. I could throw the ball. Sure, it would miss the target by a remarkable distance—enough so that people would think I was throwing the ball aside in frustration—but I could throw it nonetheless. And, if I threw a pass that defied logic and reached its intended target, I'm pretty sure I could both slap others' asses and have my own ass slapped. I still wouldn't see the point, but I could bite the bullet just to be a guy's guy.

But then, I recalled a time in my backyard in which I was pleading my side of a lost argument, while tossing a tennis ball as hard as I could against the back wall of my home. Each time I hit brick instead of windows, grass or nothingness, my confidence and throwing intensity grew. Pitch after pitch smacked against the wall and bounced back to me, with little required of me beyond a step to either side. I started getting creative, and attempted a knuckleball. I tried a curve. And a split-finger fastball. They weren't poetry, but the ball was still coming back to me. I started offering play-by-play.

"Ladies and gentlemen, what an exhibition of hurling excellence we've borne witness to this afternoon. The finish is finally coming through on this oh-so-exciting diamond in the rough. I'll tell you, Jerry, I've seen things this afternoon I didn't even know to look for. This young man is special. The last ten pitches in a row have been pure heat, utterly unhittable. Look for number eleven to be . . ."

At this point, I noticed my friend and neighbor, who makes

most hardcore bikers look like recreational cyclists, standing a dozen feet away, watching me sling tennis balls at my house. I'm not sure how long he'd been standing there, or what he'd think of me narrating my own life. I changed the subject and, after some small talk, prepared myself for the next big pitch.

I couldn't announce the play out loud anymore, but I didn't want to lose the atmosphere I'd created, so I instead ran through the play-by-play in my head.

"Ten unhittable pitches for this young, good-looking hurler. Jerry, what's next in his repertoire? A breaking ball? I've got to think he's going to follow up that fastball with a breaker. He winds, he's exploding forward, and here it comes. Straight down the middle of the . . . what the fuck?

"What the fuck!" It's an echo, but not in my voice, or announcer Jerry's. My friend, once twelve feet away, is closing in on twelve inches. I've rarely seen such fury outside of shows like *When Animals Attack.* "Why the fuck would you do that?" It took me a split second for my fear and my realization to sync up; I immediately wished they hadn't. It would seem pitch eleven left the arm of the very special young man at an angle that would lead observers to question, "How did he throw that sideways?" After that, this rapid-moving orb headed straight for a target—not *the* target, but it still moved as though on a mission. As an inanimate object, though, it couldn't know that its mission was apparently to move at a great pace until arriving at the side of my friend's neck, whereupon it would come to a sudden and not entirely graceful stop.

Very few times have I begged for my life, and never with as much vigor as at that moment. My friend could not fathom how this fuck-up couldn't have been on purpose. Ultimately, I was saved when another friend arrived and confirmed, "Yup, he really sucks that bad." Cooler heads prevailed.

More recently, when a neighbor learned of my Canadian origins, his immediate response was one I had heard many times before. "Oh, you must love fishing." I responded, "Oh, you went to school in Wisconsin. You must love grilled cheese sandwiches."

My neighbor was right. I do enjoy fishing . . . to a point. Believe it or not, though, some Canadians *don't*, just like there are at least seven who don't watch hockey. I could love fishing if somehow I could still look like a real guy without touching the bait (ever) or the fish (until it arrived with drawn butter on my plate.) Until I was an adult, I was convinced worms' rings were teeth, and the wetness on their skin was saliva from the many teeth-lined mouths. If a worm was docile, I could maybe spear it on a hook and pull my fingers away before I was bitten. But if I pulled it from a Styrofoam container and it moved, even a little, I would scream and drop it on the floor of the boat. This doesn't reek of toughness.

So when I took in a show recently about catfish noodling—in which you dangle a hand into a catfish's underwater hole and then, when the fish swallows your hand, you drag the fish up and out of the water by its gills—I shuddered. I may have even peed a little; not a full saturation, but just enough to stay cold and uncomfortable and ever aware of just how much of a pussy I am. I shuddered, I peed, and then I yelled in horror, "Patty, did you see that? Did you? Are you kidding me? Who the fuck would do that?" Whereupon she pointed out that her brother is a veteran noodler; apparently he the fuck would do that.

Fishing is one thing; hunting is another. I will never take up this sport; I lack the stomach (or the weapons) for it. Whenever I spot a deer in the woods, I never think, "What a beautiful and majestic creature. I'd sure like to blow his head clean off." It's not that I'm a radical animal lover or tree hugger. I just think these animals look more natural in the woods than on living room walls. Even if talked into a tree stand, I doubt I could pull the trigger. I'd miss, plummet to the earth, and end up with a ten-point buck's rack through my chest.

Too bad my lack of manliness isn't limited to the wilderness. Sadly, I'm equally lost whenever I encounter repair issues with cars, bicycles, appliances, and homes. If this counts toward evolution, survival of the fittest and whatnot, my kind is an endangered species. A couple of years ago, our electric garage door opener was not functioning properly and, thinking I could make my wife hot for me if I could fix it, I decided to do it myself. I almost did myself in. To do the repair I presumed was necessary, I started by detaching the spring that supports the garage door assembly against the front wall of the house. I didn't realize that these springs are under tremendous pressure, and can only be released safely after a series of precautionary measures. On the third turn of the bolt, the stress on the door caused the wood to crack, then snap violently away, then launch, in a handful of spears, to all sides of my face. To my amazement, I was unharmed, although I had almost turned an optical organ into a bloody approximation of a martini olive. I didn't soil myself, but that tentative dollop of pee was once again a tenant in my boxers.

Blaming parents for one's shortcomings is a popular fallback. But I can't fault my Dad for my complete lack of brainpower in the presence of tools (power and manual). He tried. I tried. It's just that I had an older brother who was a born do-it-yourselfer, the kind who can look at any machine, tear it apart, study it, improve it and put it back together. I'm the kind that looks at such machines and calls my brother. Given the choice between a competent child (a.k.a. a guy's guy) and another who would likely maim all parties involved (a.k.a. a sissy/liability), my father chose wisely. By default, my mother inherited me, which accounts for my ability to bake but not to build.

Like most guys, I like to kill an evening in the bar. Patty and I are members of a private club—trust me, it sounds far more exclusive and appealing than it really is—within staggering distance of our home. When I get there, though, I stand out like a severed and gangrenous thumb with eczema. I rarely play pool, darts, bag toss, poker, or any other sport-like activities. Part of the reason is that I'm invited only when another guy is depressed about a losing streak and would like me to end it. The other part of the reason is that any activity that involves using both hands, other than drinking, takes away a hand that should be involved in drinking. I know my priorities.

So how do those of us who can't live the life of an adventurer prove we're worthy of bearing (and baring) the broadsword of manliness, something so male we refer to it not as an item but as a complete concept: our manhood? I know what I do. I brush furniture-stripping gel on my hand, and then I don't wash it off until it really starts to hurt. Wincing and whining but staying the course, I sit back on my toilet with a forced smile and follow a story that seems tailor-made for me: *How to Watch Sports Like a Pro.*

Waiting for God . . . Oh

This past Saturday morning my hangover, carefully tailored over a too-long Friday evening (of which I remember little other than a niggling sense apologies were owed), delivered in spades on its excruciating promise. My eyes opened to find the familiar, virtual elephant right there at the end of my bed, filing his nails with an emery board. "Good morning, sunshine," he said, and then without warning, extended both back legs into (and through) the center of my forehead. Kathunk! My eyes slammed shut, hard enough to be audible, but the impact was not enough to shake loose the now-excited pachyderm off the dance floor he had made of my head. My elephant and I go way back.

I hadn't even had the chance to welcome the first waves of remorse, or to make the standard oath about never doing this again if the pain would just stop now, when the doorbell chimed. In my pounding, swirling cerebellum, its normally gentle tone was New Year's in October. I tried to hit my mental sleep button, but my elephant blocked me with his trunk. "Uh, no. If you do the crime . . ." I was fully prepared to do the time, but couldn't it wait until the afternoon?

Our son Connor sailed down the stairs toward for the door, as he always does. Fourteen-year-olds move at only one speed—breakneck—unless their destination is an assigned chore. Each of his heavy steps was a sucker punch to my eardrum, a blunt force trauma machine. One would think Connor had been waiting on a strip-o-gram, or expected to find a stack of gleaming gold bars on the porch with his name stamped into each. These he would spend at the gas station on seventeen thousand bags of corn chips and, to wash them down, a transport tanker of Monster drink. He would come home with no change.

More often than not, though, he found no treasure other than one of his pals. In the process of deciding what to do next, he would hold the door wide open, thus inviting the entire insect kingdom into our home to devour his mother. I, in turn, would spend the rest of my day battling both nausea and cicadas.

I eased open our bedroom door, admonishing myself for failing to saturate the shrieking hinges in WD-40, and looked down toward our entryway. Even my eyes felt bruised. I was ready to whisper-yell, "Shut the door!" but was stopped short. Unless Connor's friends had experienced profound growth spurts overnight, and celebrated their new height with the purchase of pinstriped suits and leather portfolios, these callers were not looking for him.

"Are your mom and dad home?"

Oh please, son, please, please, tell them I'm asleep. No, tell them you're an orphan. I'll give you a hundred—no, ten thousand—dollars, cash. Whatever you do, please don't let them know I'm here. Please?

"Dad? Oh, Daaaad. There's someone at the door."

I made a quick mental note to tape a bushel of peanuts all over Connor and then sic the elephant on him. For this transgression, he'd live the rest of his short life as a thin, shapeless paste. Whenever we'd go anywhere in the future, I'd simply reel him up tight like a Fruit Roll-Up and tuck him in my stinky armpit, thus adding insult to injury. At a minimum, I knew I'd soon deliver an important sermon on the merits and finer points of lying through one's teeth.

In my bathrobe, I made my way, at a more comfortable, middle-aged pace, down the stairs and to the door. The carpet sounded unusually percussive. I thought about twisting the soft skin on the back of Connor's arm on my way past, but I exercised restraint.

"Yes?" I couldn't muster enough energy to provide a more inspired response to the hearty "Good morning!" now echoing in my skull.

"Hello, I'm Pastor Busybody from the First Baptist Church of the Relentlessly Bothersome. This is my colleague, Brother Bible Thumper." These may not have been his exact words, but I'm terrible with names and it's not at all like I'd ever open the door to these same people again. "And how are you this morning?"

I thought, should I tell him? Or should I just pantomime my agony, and punctuate my answer by spearing myself in the stomach and launching a half dozen stale cocktails all over his suit? Or would he get the message that I was suffering if I extended one arm to each side of the doorframe, with one foot over the other in the middle of the doorway, and say, "Get it?"

"I'm fine." See Connor, that's how to lie. "Can I help you?"

"We're just visiting some of our neighbors in the community, and wanted to invite you to join us for Mass this Sunday."

"Oh, okay, thanks. Yeah, great." I started to close the door before my hangover would have a chance to wish an aneurysm on a man of the cloth.

He stepped forward. "Oh, one more thing?"

Frustrated, I grabbed the front of my robe, threw my arms wide open, and stood stark naked before my unwanted guests. Wiggling my hips from side to side and up and down in a barbaric variation on crossing myself, I screamed, "Who's your Moses now?"

I didn't actually do this. Instead, I just stared stupidly and hoped for a sudden cardiac arrest.

"If you were to die today . . ." I didn't tell him how close to the mark he was. "If you were to die today, would you feel comfortable knowing our Lord and Savior would be there to see you home?" I didn't tell him this, but the Lord hadn't seen me all the way home the night prior, two hours of which I spent sleeping on the neighbor's lawn.

Oh, no. I had foolishly entertained the notion that because these were Christians, and not the Jehovah's Witnesses I'd hidden from the day before, I might get off easy. Not so. I raised my left leg behind me and raked my toenails harshly down the back of my right calf, as punishment for being so unable to stand my ground and simply close the door. Why is religion sold door to door like boxes of frozen steaks? I thought this was something deeply personal, not something you could order like the set of encyclopedias you never finish buying (and, as a consequence, are well-versed in all things A to Bh but know nothing about zithers, zacatons, and zaddikim).

I've never been good at confrontation. If, at a restaurant, we receive poor service, do I get all chivalrous and browbeat the waiter for spoiling my wife's experience? No. I say, "Honey, this is completely unacceptable. Here's what we're going to do. I'm going to storm off to the bathroom and, while I'm gone, you should say something. And I'll continue to retreat to the bathroom until they set things right!" My indignation is awe-inspiring, but my balls are fluffy little cotton puffs.

Patty would be of no help to me in this instance. I couldn't say, "Hang on a sec. My wife calls all the shots about religion. She's Catholic, you know." No, Patty was sound asleep, most likely under the gentle breeze being fanned over her by my elephant. If I woke her to facilitate my own escape, I would pay dearly.

"I don't really like to talk about my faith." I inched the door forward again. "Okay?"

"Of course. But just know Jesus loves you, and He hopes you'll invite him into your heart. And please remember our church welcomes you and your family."

After a few further pleasantries, I was freed to return to my suffering.

So, based on my reaction to door-to-door faith peddling, am I a total non-believer? I don't know. I do know that I warm to the idea of organized religion about as much as I embrace the idea of the tooth fairy and the Easter bunny, neither of whom have come through for me since I was a child. I respect science, and humanity, so the concepts and rituals of a formal church offer more questions than answers. Too many atrocities are committed in the name of God (substitute Allah, or Buddha, or any other supreme being here, according to your preference) for me to embrace their tenets.

The movie *Jesus Camp* and the evangelical right have pushed me further from accepting all things divine. I could engage many of my dearest friends and family in a protracted pissing match on this subject, but I'd rather not. I respect (and even envy) their faith; I just haven't found my way toward sharing it. Suffice it to say the evidence hasn't swayed me so far. Now, if Jesus showed up at my door and spent an afternoon teaching me how to throw a ninety-five-mile-an-hour split-finger fastball, or offering tips about how to win every argument with Patty, I'd convert. Those would be miracles.

My lack of enthusiasm for organized religion wasn't for lack of trying. My parents took us to church most Sundays when we were kids. I was even an altar boy for a few years. Of course, I didn't do much to promote my future salvation by gulping back huge stacks of communion wafers and washing them down with sacramental wine (at age twelve), nor did I score points with my Mom by scratching my ass through my vestments just before serving the host to a crowd of parishioners. However, there were finer moments, as well.

I once attended a servers' retreat led by the Archbishop for our diocese. He was one of the kindest, most loving people I've ever met. He tried to teach me how to tread water during a pool visit as part of the weekend; I've still never learned, but his efforts touched me. Even if God was a mystery to me, he seemed wise and divine, so I couldn't completely dismiss faith as science fiction. Something was moving in him. The bishop even forgave me when I spilled an entire glass of grape juice on his lily-white dining room carpet. His wife, on the other hand, flashed me a look that suggested that, if she had her way, she'd be happy to shove me bodily into the depths of Hell.

As an adult, I tried to find faith, because it didn't seem to be looking for me. I read the works of C.S. Lewis (the Christian essays, not just the Narnia fantasies) and other Christian writers. Some of the arguments were compelling. I tried several churches, and a couple of bible study groups (one led, to my surprise, by a chap named Mort Goldberg). None of these offered any magic. I even prayed, once or twice, as a favor to friends who had asked me to do so in their time of need. But nothing stuck.

When Patty became sick, many people told me they were praying for my wife. I appreciated this. Just because belief doesn't come to me easily doesn't mean I want to tempt fate. Patty is in better health today. I believe this is a testament to Patty's toughness and will to live. Others may believe it was a response to prayer. Who knows? I have Patty now, so if the prayers were the reason she's still here, I owe a debt of gratitude. When I reported on a blog that Patty had been taken off the active heart transplant list, a friend with whom I'd lost touch called me out of the blue, his first such call in several years.

"So, I guess you believe in miracles now."

I felt trapped. "I don't know if I believe in miracles, but I'm sure happy Patty seems to have turned a corner."

My friend responded, "Then you're the dumbest smart guy I know."

I know my friend's heart was in the right place, and I never doubt the strength and sincerity of his faith. But I couldn't lie to him. I can lie to holy rollers who interrupt a hard-earned, high-quality hangover, but I can't readily lie to friends. I'd rather be a stupid smart guy than attempt to mislead a true believer.

My honesty about my lack of faith seems to always get me into trouble. One of my close friends told me, after a prolonged happy hour, that she found it sad that I didn't accept God's hand in our lives, and even more so that I couldn't encourage my kids to have faith. I suppose this *is* sad. It's also more than a little frightening. Believers have heaven (which, if it exists, must have some amazing restaurants) to look forward to; I have dirt and hungry worms and nothingness. Try sleeping at night when you can do the math between you and no longer you. So I try to strike a balance. I will listen to their arguments in support of their faith, and just keep my mouth shut (Patty taught me this).

Still, I always wonder. Last night, I stepped outside for a cigar. I usually watch the comings and goings of rabbits that overpopulate our lawn, or peep into my neighbors' windows to see if anyone's still up or having an impromptu romp on a kitchen table. On this occasion, though, I found myself captivated by a full moon. Here I was, standing on an enormous spinning orb teeming with countless varieties of life, staring up at another celestial body almost 240,000 miles away, surrounded on a vast canvas by stars so distant I could never reach them in many lifetimes. For sure, the science is fascinating. And yet, playing at the edges of my desire to be analytical was a sense of awe. I'm not ready to say I was looking at conclusive evidence for God, but I felt *something*.

So maybe, just maybe, there's still some hope for my jaded, atheistic and alcohol-pickled soul. I just wish it wouldn't come looking for me early on Saturday morning. Elephants never forget, and they don't like to be kept waiting.

About the Author

Brian O'Mara-Croft has wanted to be an author all his life. He submitted ideas for a novel to several publishers at age 10; good sense kept them from accepting. His unfortunate tendency to procrastinate meant his first book—this one—didn't come to fruition until he was in his early forties. He is currently writing a second collection of essays, co-authoring a book with his wife Patty about her battles with heart failure, and pondering a novel. Brian maintains a humorous blog at lostinthehive.blogspot.com, and can be contacted at brianomaracroft@yahoo.com. He lives in a suburb of Chicago.